Conversation Course

Course Book

von
Jenny Richardson-Schlötter

Ernst Klett Sprachen
Barcelona · Budapest · London · Ljubljana · Prag
Posen · Sofia · Stuttgart

Conversation Course

von

Jenny Richardson-Schlötter

1. Auflage 1 4 3 2 | 2007 06 05

Alle Drucke dieser Auflage können im Unterricht nebeneinander benutzt werden, sie sind untereinander unverändert. Die letzte Zahl bezeichnet das Jahr dieses Druckes.

Redaktion: Margit Künzel
Gestaltung: Monika Senn
Einbandgestaltung: Christine Schneyer
Illustrationen: Sepp Buchegger
Umschlagfoto: Alamy Limited / Mark Dyball
Reproduktion: Meyle + Müller,
                Medien-Management,
                Pforzheim.
Druck: W. Wirtz, Speyer
ISBN 3-12-524154-5

9 783125 241541

Introduction

Willkommen bei **On the Move** *Conversation Course*, dem praktischen Englischkurs für Fortgeschrittene!

Sicherlich haben Sie schon einige Jahre Englisch gelernt an der Volkshochschule oder an einer anderen Institution der Erwachsenenbildung und möchten Ihre Sprachkenntnisse verbessern oder auch nur auf dem Laufenden halten. Der vorliegende Kurs bietet Ihnen hierzu eine optimale Gelegenheit.

Ein reicher Fundus an interessanten und aktuellen Themen aus dem unmittelbaren Lebensumfeld bietet vielfältige Herausforderungen sich in der Zielsprache zu verständigen.

Die insgesamt 20 Themen folgen einem sog. „Jahreszeitenzyklus" (Frühling, Sommer, Herbst und Winter); pro Jahreszeit werden fünf Themen angeboten, die aber auch jederzeit außerhalb der jeweiligen Jahreszeit bearbeitet werden können.

Das Thema „O" *(First things first)* ist als ein zusätzliches Angebot zu verstehen und kann z. B. als „Starter" zum Kursbeginn eingesetzt werden. Die Abfolge in der Bearbeitung der Themen ist beliebig und kann je nach Bedürfnislage der einzelnen Kurse völlig unterschiedlich zusammengestellt werden. Dieser flexible Ansatz ermöglicht auch reibungslose Übergänge zwischen Kursen, die z. B. über zwei Semester laufen. Jedes Thema bildet eine in sich abgeschlossene Einheit und baut nicht auf der vorherigen Einheit auf.

Die Struktur der 20 thematischen Einheiten obliegt hingegen einem stringenten Schema: Jedes Thema folgt dem Doppelseitenprinzip und beinhaltet einen Hör- und Lesetext sowie vielfältige interaktive Aktivitäten, die um die Kerntexte angesiedelt sind. Außerdem gibt es pro Thema landeskundliche Informationen, die mit dem folgenden Symbol gekennzeichnet werden.

Im Anhang gibt es ein alphabetisches Wortregister, welches allerdings nicht die Arbeit mit einem „richtigen" Wörterbuch ersetzen kann und soll.

Ferner werden im Anhang alle Hörtexte abgedruckt, die vorne bei den Themen unter dem Symbol angekündigt werden. Mit der zum Kurs gehörenden integrierten CD können alle Texte auch noch einmal zu Hause gehört werden, um somit die Hörfertigkeit intensiver zu schulen.

Nicht zuletzt finden sich im Anhang die „Files", auf die vorne bei den Themen verwiesen wird. Sie sind ein zusätzliches Angebot von recht unterschiedlichen Aufgaben rund um die Zielsprache Englisch.

Als ein weiteres Sprachangebot gibt es auf der ersten Umschlaginnenseite nützliche Redewendungen, die im Unterricht aber auch außerhalb benutzt werden können.

Jetzt wünschen wir Ihnen viel Spaß und besten Erfolg mit dem
On the Move *Conversation Course!*

On the MOVE

Conversation Course

- ◆ **Course Book mit integrierter CD**
  ISBN 3-12-524154-5

- ◆ **Teacher's Book**
  ISBN 3-12-524155-3

Contents

Contents

Appendix

First things first

1   **A bus trip to Canterbury**

A   Listen. You are on a bus trip to Canterbury, England. Find a seat on the bus. For further questions look at file 1 on page 48.

Canterbury, a city in Southeast England, is over 2000 years old. It is the home of the first cathedral in England. You can also visit the Roman and early Christian ruins, a Norman castle, several museums and other attractions. The city centre is enclosed on three sides by medieval walls and many of the original Tudor houses are still standing today. Although Canterbury only has a population of 35,000, the centre is often crowded. That's because, after London, it is the most visited town in England.

2   **Circle introductions**

A   Sit in a circle and introduce someone in the circle.

This is Sandra.
She is a tour guide.
She likes to go to
Italy on holiday.
In her free time she
plays the trumpet
in a band.
She always takes
her mobile and a
good map on trips.

This is Chris, our bus driver. She drives quite fast and she loves Belgian chocolates.

3 The name game

A Use the information you have learned about the members of the class to write a little name poem for other people in the class.

Examples:

Sunny days
And
Nice people
Dreams of
Romantic sunsets
And trumpets.

Chocolate
Hiking in the mountains
Red
Italian wine
Sleeping late.

4 The Dos and Don'ts of adult education classes

A Pairwork. This is an article about adult education classes. Fill in *Do* or *Don't*.

The Dos and Don'ts of Adult Education Classes

The adult education classes are starting! Here are some tips for you.

_Do_ try to come on the first evening.
Don't be late every week. Sometimes you can't help it.
_Do_ join in the conversation.
Don't talk all the time. Let the others have a chance.
Don't bring food to class every week.
Don't be afraid of the teacher, she/he won't bite.
Don't wear a bikini unless it is a swimming class.
Don't be afraid to laugh. Humour makes learning easier.

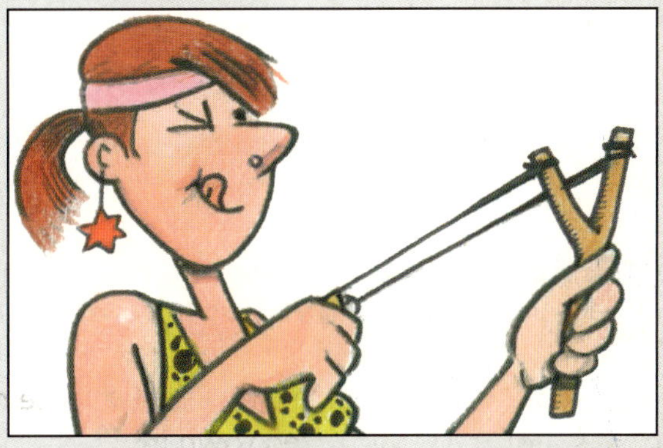

Don't worry about mistakes, the main thing is to speak.
_Do_ have fun! Enjoy yourself.

> mistake: sth that you do wrong
> unless: except if

B Do you agree with this advice? Can you think of some other *Dos* and *Don'ts*?

Do _____ ...
Don't _____ ...

Brand new or second-hand?

1 Shop till you drop   *bis zum Umfallen*

A Where would you buy the following items? Look at file 28 on page 59.

a A computer mouse
b A dress or suit for a special occasion
c A present for a friend who likes antiques
d A pair of cowboy boots for a theatre production
e An airline ticket   *at the airport*

B Group work.   Look at the mind map on page 59. Write down three or four items that you might buy at each place. Discuss the advantages and disadvantages of each place. Make a note of them in the mind map.

> I'd buy a … at a … because it is …

> What I like about … is that you …

> The (dis)advantage of … is that …

> That's the problem with …

C Report your results to the class.

D Group work.   Have you ever returned something you bought that didn't work? Was it easy or was it a problem? Do you enjoy shopping or do you find it difficult?

2 Lost and found

A Group work.   These words all appear in a story. What do you think happened?

cup   Christmas   flea market   forget-me-nots   hobby   move   mysterious   treasure

B Tell the others your story.

C Listen to the story. Have you inherited anything you use on special occasions?

D Group work.   What do you think?
1. Do you enjoy going to flea markets, second-hand shops or antique shops? Why / why not?
2. Have you ever bought anything at one of these places?
3. Have you ever tried to sell your things?
4. Have you ever lost anything and found it again?
5. Do you have something from a relative or a friend that you treasure?
6. What is it? What does it look like?

> I enjoy going to … because …

> Once I bought a … at a …

> I lost my … at the … but luckily I found it.

> You're kidding! That was lucky! How did you find it?

3 A treasure or a white elephant?

An elephant is sometimes considered holy in India, Sri Lanka, Thailand and Burma. An elephant requires much care and is quite expensive for the owner to keep, but it is not very useful. To-day the word "white elephant" is used to describe something that is of little use to the owner, but may be of use to someone else. For example, you may have received a vase for a present and you think it is ugly, but someone else might like it.

A Think of something you have at home, but don't really want anymore. It may be in your attic or basement or under your bed. It may be a white elephant. Now is your chance to sell or trade or give it away in class. Write an ad for one or two items on a piece of paper. Include a short description and price.

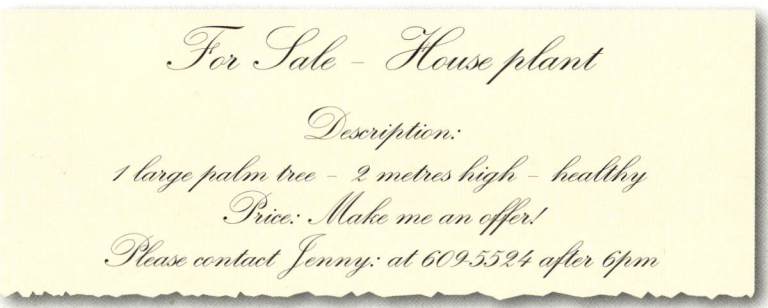

For Sale - House plant

Description:
1 large palm tree - 2 metres high - healthy
Price: Make me an offer!
Please contact Jenny: at 609-5524 after 6pm

B Now put your ad up on the wall and then look at the other ads. Go shopping around your classroom.

> I'm interested in your …

> How much would you like for it?

> Why are you selling it?

> Well, I'll think about it.

4 Show and tell

"Show and tell" is a popular tradition in US schools. Students are asked to bring things they are interested in to class and talk about them. Your class can do it, too!

Bring something to class next week and tell the others about it.
It can be a thing you inherited or bought or maybe it was a present you received.
It can be a picture or photographs or part of a collection.
It can be something you use for your hobby, a piece of clothing or anything.

2 St. Patrick's Day

1 Green Buffet

Help yourself – I made a …

What other foods are green?

You might call it lime green.

2 Ireland Quiz

A Read all about St. Patrick in file 3 on page 48.

B Pairwork. Read the quiz with your partner and mark your answers.

1. The official language of Ireland is …
   Irish English ☒
   Irish and English ☒
   Irish Gaelic ☐
   English ☐

2. Which instrument is not traditional?
   harp *Harfe* ☒
   ? tin whistle *Blech Flöte* ☐
   guitar ☒
   ? bodhrán *Trommel* ☐
   (Tischecke)

Minister → 3. What does Taoiseach mean?
   prime minister ☒
   a traditional Irish meal ☐
   a county in the west ☐
   good luck ☐

4. When you kiss the Blarney Stone, you …
   will have a long happy life. ☒
   may be lucky and find a pot of gold. ☐
   will be given the gift of eloquent speech. ☒
   will find your true love soon. ☐

5. Which of these sports is the national sport?
   golf ☐
   tennis ☐
   Gaelic football ☒
   Irish dancing ☐

6. St. Patrick's Day was celebrated in
   New York in 1711 ☐
   Boston in 1737 ☒
   Jamestown in 1699 ☐
   Miami in 1969 ☐

7. People don't … on St. Patrick's Day.
   sing traditional songs ☐
   drink green beer ☐
   have parades ☒
   give presents ☒

8. What is a leprechaun?
   a small mouse-like animal ☐
   a mischievous elf ☒
   a bright yellow flower ☐
   a type of cake ☐
   Papageientaucher

9. If you see a puffin, you see an unusual
   mammal ☐
   fish ☐
   insect ☐
   bird ☒

10. Before the Irish take a drink, they
    state "Guinness is good for you". ☐
    say "Slainte". *(Slainche)* *Prost* ☒
    wink at the others and smile. ☐
    shout "Down the hatch". ☐

B Check your answers with your teacher.

3 Leprechauns

Lepecorns

A Listen to the man talking about leprechauns. Number the questions in the order he answers them.

1. How do you catch a leprechaun and what do you get?
2. What do they look like?
3. When did you first hear of leprechauns?
4. What do leprechauns do ?

B Listen again and check your answers. Read a story about a leprechaun in file 4 on page 48.

C Group work.   Discuss.

1. How many fantasy characters can you name from books, television or legends?
2. When you were young did you hear any stories about fairies, elves, rabbits or other such imaginary people?
3. Do you think it is a good idea to tell children these stories? Why/why not? Do you remember when you realized they may not be true?
4. Did you have a favourite story or book when you were a child?
5. Why do you think people like fantasy and science fiction books and films? Do you have a favourite?
6. If you caught a leprechaun, what would you wish for?

> I'm interested in what people imagine the future will be like.

> I'd wish for him to clean my house.

> I used to love reading fairy tales, but now …

4 I'll tell Me Ma

A Turn to file 5 on page 49. Use the words in the box to complete the popular folk song from Belfast. Listen to the song to check your answers and sing along.

zehc

| home | still | her | comb | toes | she | apple pie | own | die | City | well | sky |

komm

5 Those funny little green men

A Group work.   How many words can you make out of the letters in the word leprechauns?

3 The Red Hatters – Mad Hatters?

1 Older and wiser?

A Group work.   True or false? Explain. Rewrite the sentences to make them true.

1. Young people today respect the older generation more.
2. Parents should put their children first until they are grown up.
3. Grandparents should always be ready to help with grandchildren.
4. Different generations should live together.
5. Older people shouldn't wear fashionable clothes. They should look their age.
6. The older generation is always more conservative than the younger generation.
7. Grandparents can't teach their grandchildren a lot. Things have changed too much.
8. You are too old to learn anything new after 60.

> I don't think that's right …

> That's right, but when are they grown up?

> Why do you say that?

> What do you mean by fashionable clothes?

> Maybe for …, but you are not too old to …

2 "Getting older is not so bad."

A   Read the article. What is the missing word?

The Red Hat Society

You'll look twice when you see them. Maybe you'll look three or four times. It's OK with them. Smile and laugh with them. They are having …

So, who are they? The Red Hat Society, a group of older, <u>bolder</u> women who wear purple outfits with red hats in public and don't care what other people think. Sue Cooper started the club a few years ago after she read a poem called "Warning" by Jenny Joseph. Now there are more than 6,000 clubs worldwide.

Who are the Red Hatters and what do they do?

The answer is simple. They are women and the <u>purpose</u> of the group is to have ….

There are no <u>fund-raising projects</u>, no business meetings and no <u>rules</u>. Well, almost.

To join the Red Hat Society, a woman must be 50 or older and must wear a red hat and purple outfit to all the meetings and social events. Younger women can also join and they wear pink hats and lavender <u>outfits</u>.

In most women's clubs, the activities are mainly <u>volunteer work</u> at hospitals, old people's homes or at schools. They also work hard raising money for people and institutions in need. The Red Hat Society is different.

It is just for … Their activities include going to the movies together, to concerts or museums or out for tea.

Some of the women enjoy <u>dressing up</u>, because life is very

informal in the US today. This is a chance to look nice, wear a dress and hat.

Mary Bagly explains why she likes the club, "Most of us have been conservative all our lives. This gives us an eccentric, … thing to do."

Lily Sayers says: "I enjoy the club because it's a chance for women of different generations to meet and have … I think it is also important because it shows younger people that getting older is not so bad."

bold: not frightened of taking risks
dress up: to wear formal clothes for a special occasion
fund-raising: collecting money for a particular purpose
outfit: a set of clothes for a particular event
rule: an official instruction about what you must or must not do
volunteer work: to work without being paid

3 What do you think?

1. Would you join a club like this? Why or why not?
2. What kinds of clubs do you have in your area?
3. Why do people join clubs?
4. Are you a member of a club? Which one?
5. Does it have rules? Meetings? Dues? Fund-raising activities? Explain.
6. Do you have special clothes that you wear to the meetings?
7. What kinds of clubs have a uniform? Why?

> Yes, I think it sounds like fun.

> People join clubs so they can …

> We raise money by selling …

> I'm a member of …

About 59 million people in the US did volunteer work in 2002. This means one in four persons over 16 volunteered some of their time. In the US churches are not supported, so they have to be self-financing. This explains the high number of volunteers in this area, 34%. The next largest group, 27%, volunteered in schools or in organizations which support young people. About 12% worked in social services and 9% worked for health organizations. In Britain volunteering is also a way of life. You can volunteer at the National Trust where you might help with renovating an historic site.

4 Future plans

A What would you like to do when you retire?

> I'd like to go …

> I hope I'll be able to …

B Some people are talking about their future. Underline the things you think they will mention.

| family | travel | work | health | money | sports | learning |

C Listen. Which things did they mention?

D Group work. Discuss.

1. Is there someplace you would like to travel to? Would you like to go on a long trip?
2. Did your parents choose your job for you? How did you decide?
3. Is there anything you would like to learn more about? How can you do it?
4. Do you have a volunteer job? Do you think it is a good idea? Do you know about any volunteer jobs?

4 Earth Day

1 Birds of a feather flock together

A Listen to your teacher. She/He will say two words and point to two different corners of the room. Which word attracts you? Go to that corner and say why.

2 Natural Wonders

A Group work. If you were to choose seven natural wonders, which ones would you choose?

B Compare your list with the others in the class.

C Read the interview in file 6 on page 49 and answer the questions.

1. Have you visited any of these places?
2. Are there any areas around here that are protected?
3. What problems arise when conservationists try to protect more land?

3 How well do you know the plant world?

A Pairwork. Read the statements with your partner and find the answers.

(The answers to two to six are in the box.)

1. Which of the plants in the box can you find above?

   bamboo, begonias, chrysanthemums, daffodils, ferns, forget-me-nots, heather, geraniums, orchids, petunias, roses, sequoia tree, tulips, water lilies

2. This member of the grass family is from China and can grow as much as 1.2 metres a day.
3. This is the tallest tree in the world. It is over 117 metres and grows in northern California.
4. This is one of the oldest plants on earth and grows in tropical climates as well as areas north of the Arctic Circle.
5. The pods of this flower are vanilla beans which are used to produce vanilla flavouring in foods.
6. The name of this flower comes from a Turkish word which means turban.

B Check the answers in class.

4 What do you think?

A **Group work.** **Discuss.**

> I have a friend who speaks English to her plants.

> I enjoy visiting botanical gardens.

> I remember eating raspberries in my grandmother's garden.

1. Do you enjoy working in the garden?
2. Have you got a favourite flower or plant?
3. Do certain flowers have a special meaning?
4. Have you ever visited a famous garden or park?
5. Do you have any house plants?
6. Do you have any tips for taking care of plants?
7. Do you believe in talking to your plants and playing music to help them grow?
8. Do you remember any gardens from your childhood? What were they like?

aches / pains — Schmerzen

5 Herbal medicines

A **Group work.** For thousands of years people have used plants and herbs to make medicines to cure their aches and pains. Match the herbal <u>remedy</u> to these aches and pains.

Schwarzahn

1. <u>sage</u> Salbei	a 4	arthritis
2. lavender tea	b 5	burns – Verbrennung
3. <u>ginger</u> Ingwer	c 6	a cold
4. <u>dandelion</u> tea	d 2	a <u>hangover</u>
5. aloe vera	e 1	a sore throat
6. echinacea	f 3	travel sickness

> **dandelion:** a yellow wild flower
> **ginger:** a pale brown root with a strong taste used as a spice in cooking
> **hangover:** If you have a hangover, you feel ill, because you drank too much alcohol the evening before.
> **remedy:** sth that makes you better
> **sage:** a herb used to give flavour to food

> … might be good for travel sickness.

> I've read/heard that …

> I didn't know that.

B **Group work.** **Discuss.**

1. Do you know of any other herbal remedies?
2. Have you tried any herbal remedies?
3. Do you think they help?

> I don't believe those things are effective.

> My grandmother used to …

> I think it worked. I felt better.

> I've tried …

5 *Memories and monuments*

1 The time capsule mystery

A time capsule is a weather-proof box containing things from a certain time and place. It is usually put away in some safe place for about 100 years. Then it is opened on the 100th anniversary.

A **Group work.** What would you expect to find in a box that was put together 100 years ago? If you were making up a box of things to be opened in 100 years, what would you put in? Think of eight items.

> They might have put in ...

> I'd put in ...

B Read the article. What is the mystery? Are some of the things you mentioned in A in the box?

Time Capsule Mystery in Portland, Oregon

One hundred years ago President Theodore Roosevelt rode into Portland in a <u>carriage</u>, <u>made a speech</u> about the great <u>pioneers</u> and put a <u>copper box</u> into the cornerstone of a monument to Lewis and Clark. These two men were the first to find the way across the northern US to the Pacific Ocean.

They started their <u>expedition</u> in May of 1804 and ended it in 1806.

Now the president's great-grandson, Theodore Roosevelt IV, plans to read the same speech, stand on the same hill and open the old box, filled with relics of American life in 1903. That is, he will open it, if anyone can find it. People in Portland cannot find the time capsule. Nobody knows exactly where it is.

The problem is that after the box was <u>buried</u> there was a square built around the monument, so now people don't know if the box is under the monument, just north of it, or maybe a little to the south, east or west.

But we do know what is in the box, because there was a list of the items in the newspaper the day after Roosevelt's visit. There are historical documents, maps, stories about people living in the area, wood from an Oregon tree, a two-cent stamp, three pennies, information about Portland and its schools, a piece of rock salt, and a portrait of Roosevelt. If they don't find it in time, Mr

Roosevelt will read his great-grandfather's speech and make one of his own. Then we will ask people to give us things from their pockets or <u>purses</u> for a new time capsule.

This time the historical society will write the exact location of the time capsule and give the information to the newspapers.

So one hundred years from now someone should be able to find the time capsule!

> **bury:** to put sth in the ground
> **carriage:** vehicle with wheels pulled by a horse
> **expedition:** an organized journey for a special purpose
> **make a speech:** a formal talk that s.o. gives to a group of people
> **pioneer:** one of the first people to do sth
> **purse:** handbag (AE)

C What do you have with you in your pockets or bag that could be put in a time capsule? Find eight to ten items for your personal class time capsule.

2 Sacagawea, Bird Woman

In 1999, the US treasury introduced a dollar coin with a picture of another member of Lewis and Clark's expedition. Her name was Sacagawea, a Native American. Little is known about her, but we do know that she was only a teenager when she acted as their guide, translator and a bridge between cultures. Without her bravery, knowledge and help Lewis and Clark might never have found the Northwest Passage. Her baby son was born on this expedition.

A **Listen to two people talking about Sacagawea. Which words describe which person or thing?**

adventurous amazing	brilliant brave	dead boring dry	exciting fantastic	fascinating intelligent	interesting sensible

1. Sacagawea   2. Diary   3. History at school
4. A film about the exploration of the Antarctic   5. A book about a Mount Everest expedition

B **Group work.** **We know a little about Sacagawea's life because William Clark mentioned her in his diary.**

1. Do you/Have you ever kept a diary?
2. Are diaries popular today? Have you ever read a famous diary?
3. Do you enjoy watching films about different countries? Have you seen one recently?
4. Do you enjoy reading books about real-life adventures?
5. Do you think it is important to write down your own personal history? Why/why not?
6. Has anyone in your family written down your family's history?
7. Do you remember a story told to you by any of your relatives?

> My … told me a story about when …

> I saw a film recently about …

> I keep a diary of all my trips.

> Oh, do you put in pictures?

3 Monuments

A **Group work.** **What do you think these statues honour? Discuss and report your thoughts to the others. Then read about the statues in file 7 on page 50.**

4 What do you think?

1. Is there a monument in your town?
2. Who or what does it honour and why?
3. Do you think monuments are meaningful? Why / why not?
4. Which person or what event would you like to see honoured?
5. How would you like to see the person honoured? (with a coin, a statue, a stamp, a street name or something else)
6. Can you think of a stamp or coin that you like because of the person or thing on it?

> I think there should be a monument of … because that's what this town is famous for.

> There is a monument dedicated to …

> I like the Italian Euro coins, because …

6 *Something old, ...*

Something old, something new, something borrowed, something blue. This is a traditional piece of advice for <u>brides</u>. For good luck they should wear something old (passed down in the family), something new (to symbolize a new start), something borrowed (usually from a friend) and something blue. In biblical days blue symbolized purity.

Biblische Tage

1 An old-fashioned fairy tale?

Or is it a modern tale? Does it have a happy ending? The story got mixed up. Arrange the sentences into a story. You can use as many sentences as you like. You can add some details if you like.

A **Pairwork.** **Start your story with:**

Once upon a time there were two people.
Her name was *Diana*
His name was *Charles*
She was *19* years old.
He was *a son for Queen of England*
She lived in *London*
He *was the Prince of Wales*

in lived Buckingham Palace
They married in the 1981
They had two son's, Willem and Harry

B **Read your story to the class.** *Wilhelm the first one*
They got divorced in the 1996
And in 1997 she had an accident and she died

2 Be a perfect wedding guest *Charles married new wife*

They planned a wedding.
They met each other's families.
They went on a long holiday together.
They went out together.
He/She had a change of heart.
They met on an internet dating website.
They fell in love.
They went on a honeymoon.
He/She had an affair.
They lived together.
They got divorced.
She/They got pregnant.
They met at a party.
They got married.
They/She had a baby.
He/She/They lived happily ever after.

A **Read the article. Fill in the missing words. Circle the ones you agree with.**

Be a Perfect **Wedding Guest**

It's June and it is the wedding season again. Follow **Ms Eti Quette's** ten tips and you will be the perfect guest.

- Remember this is a very special day for the ___*bride*___ and groom.
- Guests can wear any colour, even the bride can wear ___*black*___
- Send your ___*present*___ to the bride before the big day. It may get lost on the wedding day.
- Never give ___*money*___.

A personal gift is best.
- Make sure you are not ___*late*___ _____ Be at the church or <u>registry office</u> at least ten minutes early.
- Ask if you can take ___*pictures*___ during the ceremony or at the <u>reception</u>.
- Congratulate the bride and groom with a big ___*kiss*___ .
- Talk to ___*guests*___ who are alone. Introduce yourself to people you don't know.
- Don't tell <u>embarrassing</u> _____ ___*stories*___ about the bride or groom at the wedding reception.
- And never drink too much and ___*dance*___ .

black
bride
dance
guests
kiss
late
money
pictures
present
stories

embarrassing: making you feel shy or ashamed
etiquette: rules about what is polite and correct behaviour
reception: a formal party that is given to celebrate a special event
registry office: a place where you can get married and where marriages are officially recorded

1. Do you agree with all the tips?
2. Is it the same in your country? What's different?
3. What advice would you add? *Zusatz*

> I would give the couple ....

> So would I.

> I wouldn't take pictures ....

> Neither would I.

> I agree with number ....

> So do I.

> I don't agree with number three.

> Neither do I.

3   Two weddings and a flat tyre

A   Which words in the box go with which picture?

big family wedding
champagne
cider
expensive
formal
first marriage
inexpensive
informal
non-traditional
second marriage
small wedding
traditional

B   Listen to the people talk about their weddings. Draw a line from the words in the middle to the wedding they describe.

4   What do you think?

> Once I went to a wedding in Japan.

> What was it like?

A   Group work.   Discuss the questions.

1. Have you been to a wedding lately? What was it like? (clothes, ceremony, reception, food, guests)
2. Have you been to a wedding in a different country? What was it like?
3. Have you been to an unusual wedding?
4. What kind of wedding gift would you give to a young couple?/ a couple who is getting married for the second time? A couple who lives in another country?
5. What are some wedding traditions in your country? Do you think they are old-fashioned or do you like them?
6. Do you think people spend too much money on big weddings nowadays?
7. Do you think marriage is important today?
8. Do you think a marriage contract is a good idea?

> I'd give someone who lived in another country something typically German.

> Like what?

> Where I come from it's still traditional to kidnap the bride.

> I don't like that custom. It's old-fashioned.

7 *Berry Good*

1 How many ways are there to eat an ice cream cone?

A **Group work.** Explain how you eat an ice cream cone. Did you do it differently when you were a child? How do you eat the following things: an egg, pizza, bread, a pancake, something you really like and something you don't like.

2 Eating in and out

A **Pairwork.** Interview your partner.

1. What kinds of food do you cook?
   a) Italian   d) German
   b) Mexican   e) Greek
   c) Chinese   f) Anything else?

2. What don't you like about other people using your kitchen?
   a) They are messy.
   b) They put things back in the wrong place.
   c) The kitchen gets too <u>crowded</u>.
   d) All of these.
   e) I don't mind if other people cook with me.

3. How do you rate your own cooking?
   a) I can barely <u>boil</u> water.
   b) I can cook the foods I like.
   c) My cooking is brilliant, I should have my own TV programme.

4. What is the worst mistake a guest can make?
   a) Not calling to say if they can come.
   b) Cancelling at the last moment.
   c) Bringing a pet.
   d) Bringing an uninvited person.

5. What do you do when you invite guests to your home?
   a) Try something new and exotic.
   b) Cook something simple, that I've made before.
   c) Get some <u>takeaway</u> food.
   d) Have a <u>potluck</u>.

6. What drives you crazy in a restaurant?
   a) Poor service

   b) Noisy atmosphere
   c) Smoking
   d) Something else?

7. What's your favourite restaurant?
   a) Medium priced place that serves good food.
   b) An ethnic restaurant.
   c) An expensive place.
   d) Your favourite?

8. What is your favourite snack?
   a) Carrots, or something healthy.
   b) Chocolate, or anything sweet.
   c) Chips, or anything salty.
   d) Something else?

9. What's your favourite dessert?
   a) Ice cream   d) I don't like dessert.
   b) cake   e) Something else?
   c) fruit

10. Do you know any tips for healthy eating?
    a) Yes, I read you should.
    b) I think it is a good idea to …
    c) No, I don't, sorry.

11. If you wrote a cookbook what would it be called?
    a) The Creative Cook
    b) Mom's Favourites
    c) Quick and Easy Meals
    d) Alternatives to Cooking
    e) Your personal title?

12. Write your own question.

boil: to heat to 100 degrees Centigrade
crowded: very full of people
potluck: everyone brings something
takeaway: a meal that you buy in a restaurant but eat at home

I'd say b and c.

I usually …

I hate it when …

I like … best.

B Group work.   Report on the interview.

3 **Guess what?**

A Group work.   Your teacher will give you a topic. Act out or draw some of the things related to the topic. The group that guesses your word correctly gets a point.

B Now can you guess what category each group has?

4 **The no-cook cook**

A Group work.   Which of these ingredients would you expect to find together in a recipe for a starter, a main course and a dessert?

blueberries	blackberries	chicken	couscous	honey
lettuce	marscapone	mayonnaise	melon	raspberries
roasted marinated vegetables		shortbread biscuits		yoghurt

B Listen and make a note of which ingredients go together.

C Check your answers with the recipes in file 13 on page 53.

5 **What do you say?**

a) Have you ever had any kitchen disasters?
b) Have your eating habits changed over the last years?
c) Would you try any of the recipes on page 53?
d) Would you follow the recipes or change them in any way?
e) Do you know any no-cook recipes?
f) Plan a menu with no-cook recipes for your class.

I used to eat at work, now I eat at home.

One time I tried to … and I forgot to …

I'd make the … differently. How?

8 *Something special*

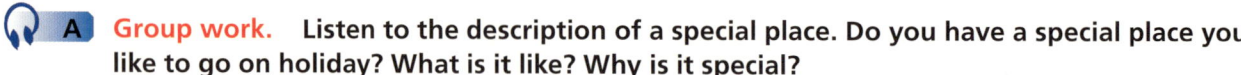

1 There's something special about the place

A **Group work.** Listen to the description of a special place. Do you have a special place you like to go on holiday? What is it like? Why is it special?

B Your teacher will give you some cards. Put the card into three groups at three different tables. Then sit at one table.

C Read out the words on your cards. Can you add any more?

> I think … and … go together.

> This word belongs in that group.

> Do you know what … means?

Kiwis are … *(More than one answer is correct.)*
a) birds that makes a sound like "kiwi, kiwi, kiwi"
b) people who come from New Zealand
c) another name for the new Zealand dollar
d) a type of fruit originally from China

Check file 9 on page 51 for the answer.

2 What's so special?

A **Group work.** Write a list of things that are special about your country. Remember you can name special foods, people, places, animals, plants, sports, types of food or anything else.

B Read your list to the class.

3 Leaving home and homecoming

On page 23 you'll read a poem about the feelings of a person who leaves her home in Jamaica and goes back to visit.

A Which words describe positive feelings sor things which are negative in your opinion. Some might be both.

You're Leaving by <u>Ochigirl</u>

You have no choice
You're scared
<u>confused</u>
Yet ....
There's excitement
<u>anticipation</u>

You Arrive ...
It's cold
<u>Overwhelming</u>
It's new
you <u>explore</u>
you experience
you <u>acclimate</u>

10 Years later you return
the air
the stars
the smell, things you <u>took for granted</u>
the people
their <u>honesty</u>
their beauty
their language ... is you

<u>Reluctantly</u> you leave
BUT with the <u>realization</u> that you
will one day return

For good.

> **acclimate:** start to feel happy with s.th.
> **anticipation:** thinking about something before it happens
> **confused:** not clear
> **explore:** to go to a place you have never been in order to find out about it
> **honesty:** truthfulness
> **overwhelming:** very strong effect
> **realization:** know something
> **reluctantly:** not wanting to
> **take for granted:** forget that you are lucky to have

 Although English is the official language of Jamaica, islanders usually speak a patois (a dialect) which is a mixture of English, Spanish and various North African languages.

B **Read the poem again and answer the questions.**

1. What does she appreciate when she goes home?
2. Does she identify with these things?
3. Do you think she will return to her home country someday?
4. Will it be easy for her to go back?
5. Where do you think she went to live? Why?

4 What do you think?

A **Group work.** **Discuss.**

1. When you come home from a holiday what do you look forward to?
2. If you went away to live in another country for a longer time, what would you take with you?
3. What things would you have to do if you moved to a different country?
4. What things that you can't take with you, would you miss ?
5. Which traditions from home would you teach your children? (language, holiday, traditions, eating habits, values, ...) Why? Do you think it would be difficult?

> I look forward to seeing my friends.

> I'd take some ... with me.

> I would teach my children ...

> I would have to ...

> I'd miss ...

9 *And the living is easy*

1 Ah, summer!

A **Which words describe the weather in the summer time in your area?**

boiling   changeable   cool   agreeably warm   mild   sticky   unbearably humid   hot   wet

B **The following text is from a book called "Notes from a Big Country" written by Bill Bryson. Check the questions he answers in the text. Make a note of the answers.**

1. What is the weather like where you live?
2. What sounds do you associate with summer?
3. Do you have a favourite place in your home in the summer?
4. Which foods do you enjoy in the summer?
5. What do you enjoy doing in the summer?
6. What annoys you about the summer?

In New England, a friend here recently explained to me, there are three times of year. Either winter has just been, or winter is coming, or it's winter.
I know what he meant. Summers here are short – they start on the first of June and end on the last day of August, and the rest of the time you had better know where your <u>mittens</u> are – but for the whole of those three months the weather is agreeably warm and nearly always sunny. […]
A screened porch is a kind of summer room on the side of the house, with walls made of fine but <u>sturdy</u> <u>mesh</u> to keep out insects. They give you all the advantages of being outdoors and indoors at the same time. They are wonderful and will always be associated in my mind with summer things – corn on the cob, watermelon, the nighttime chirr of <u>crickets</u>, […]
So when we came to the States, the one thing I asked for in a house was a screened porch, and we found one. I live out there in the summer. I am writing this on the screened porch now, staring out on a sunny garden, listening to twittering birds and the hum of a neighbour's lawn-mower, caressed by a light breeze and feeling pretty <u>darned chipper</u>.
We will have our dinner out here tonight […] and then I will lounge around reading until bedtime, listening to the crickets and watching the cheery blink of fireflies. Summer wouldn't be summer without this.

cricket: insect that makes noise
darned chipper: just fine
mesh: net
mittens: you wear them on hands to keep warm
sturdy: very strong

C **Pairwork.** **Now interview your partner using the questions in 1/B. Complete the sentence below.**

Summer wouldn't be summer without …

2 A cinquain, a poem with five lines

A **Pairwork.** Listen to your teacher.

1. _____
2. _____
3. _____
4. _____
5. _____

B Read your cinquain to the others.

3 A summer friend

A a) These words are all used to describe a smell. Rank them in order from positive to negative.

| disagreeable | not so bad | revolting | strong | sweet |

b) Think of something these things describe.

B Now you will hear the rest of the story "Ah, summer! "by Bill Bryson. He describes an experience he had while sitting on his porch one night. What animals does he mention?

C Number these phrases in the order you hear them.

a) The most effective treatment is …
b) Only here's the thing.
c) Well, it's not so bad. I don't know what all the fuss is about.
d) All this went through my mind …
e) … is absolutely the worst thing that can happen to you.
f) To show my appreciation I …

D Listen again and check your answers.

4 What's your experience?

A **Group work.** Discuss.

a) What kind of wildlife lives in your area?
b) Have you ever had an experience with an animal? What happened?
c) Have you ever seen a wild animal in its natural habitat? Where?
d) Is there an animal you would like to see?
e) Do you have any pets? What are they like?
f) What are the advantages and disadvantages of having pets?

10 *Have you got the travel bug?*

1 Travel blogs

A Travel blogs are like postcards from cyberspace. They are internet diaries which often include photos. You can find thousands on the web. Read the following blogs and decide which of the words below you would use to describe these holidays? Why?

adventurous	fun	exciting	peaceful	risky
dangerous	educational	fascinating	relaxing	strenuous

Travel blogs

August 28th Since my earliest childhood, my family has spent summers at a beach house near a small town on the Californian coast. It's a run-down wooden place with lots of worn uncomfortable furniture. It's quiet, no TV, no telephone, no microwave. Just a pair of binoculars to watch the sea lions and the whales playing in the foamy waves. Oh, and not to forget the old wet suits and surf boards in the cellar. It is always lots of fun trying to squeeze into a tiny wet suit and to "surf" in the freezing water. It's a two mile walk along the rocky beach to the nearest shop. We return every day with the newspaper, groceries and a pocket full of shells, rocks and, if we are lucky, a sand dollar. I love being here and have many fond memories of the place - the good times with my family and friends. Wish you were here.

February 4th The next day was considerably improved: lovely hot water, clean dry clothes, and fantastic weather for London in February: dry, bright, sunny, not even cold. We went to Portobello Road and enjoyed the quirky antique shops on an empty, tourist-free, non-market day. Portobello Road Market is famous, but also jam-packed on Saturdays. In the afternoon we went on a Sherlock Holmes walking tour which was fantastic – you know I'm a fan of that type of thing. Later that evening we walked around Chinatown, had a yummy dinner and went to see a play. Wish you were here!

Journal entry, July 14, 7.48 pm. Right now I'm very nervous, not afraid – terrified, actually. I'm up in my tree house, a type of hotel room here, in Kibale National Park. It's perfectly dark outside, and I'm hearing things – not just little insects – but big, large things – moving around outside. Something is crashing through the bushes just 30 ft away from my tree house. A loud snort! I hope I am dreaming. No, well, maybe it's a water buffalo? I hope it's not a …. Oh, no – more crashing! Heaven help me – an elephant right out front of my tree house just blasted her trumpet! It made a tremendous noise! I almost jumped out of my skin. You've got to be kidding! – A shot just rang out. Poachers? Wait – the elephants are breaking trees! Damn big ones, too! And here I am sitting in one! Got to go! Wish you were here!!!!

B Find words or phrases in the text that mean the same:

Beach blog
1. Another word for a place in bad condition is …
2. If it's very cold it is …
3. If something is very small, it is …

London blog
1. An unusual antique shop, it is …
2. A crowded place is …
3. A delicious meal is …

African blog
1. If you are extremely afraid, you are …
2. A very large noise is a … noise.
3. If you were frightened suddenly by a loud noise, you might say "…"

C What is your experience?

> It depends. I would if I went …

> I'd love to … sometime.

1. Can you use any of the words in A or B to describe one of your holidays?
2. Can you use any of the words in B to describe something you have experienced?
3. Which of the holidays would you enjoy? Have you ever been on a holiday like one of the ones described? When? Where?
4. What other things do you enjoy doing on holiday? Where would you go on your dream holiday?
5. Are travel blogs interesting or a waste of time? Would you write one?

> We used to …

2 Pack it light!

A Everyone is talking about going away. But first you have to pack. And packing can be a pain. Listen to the tips from a travel writer. Match the words and phrases in the box to the things she talks about. Listen again and take notes. Then compare notes.

1. plastic bags
2. suitcases
3. shoes
4. clothes
5. emergency kit

a corkscrew	roll them
for a wet bathing suit	scissors
not heavy	see-through
only two colours	sturdy
only two pairs	wheels are great

B Pairwork. Discuss.

1. What do you think of these tips?
   Do you do any of these things?
2. Do you have any personal tips for travelling light?
3. What should someone travelling to your country bring?
4. What would you recommend that they visit?
5. What do you have in your emergency kit?

3 Holiday debate

A Pairwork. Partner A looks at file 15 on page 54 and B looks at file 8 on page 50.

B Tell the others what kind of holiday you like.

11 *Do-it-yourself!*

1 Words of wisdom?

A **Group work.** Do you agree with the quotes? Why or why not? Write your own words of wisdom.

"If you want something done right, do it yourself." (Proverb)

"You must do the thing you think you cannot do." (Eleanor Roosevelt)

"All work and no play makes Jack a dull boy." (Proverb)

> That's right, because …

> Can you think of an example?

2 Habitat for Humanity

A **Group work.** Use the information on the organization, *Habitat for Humanity*. Read and report to the other groups.

Group 1: Look at file 11 on page 51.
Group 2: Look at file 14 on page 53.
Group 3: Look at file 16 on page 54.
Group 4: Look at file 19 on page 55.

Group 5: Look at file 25 on page 58.

B Listen to Chris talk about his job at *Habitat for Humanity*, in Americus, Georgia. Number the pictures in the order he talks about them.

C Listen again and mark the sentences *true* or *false*.

1. Chris is a tour guide, who visits the Global Village often.
2. In the Global Village you can experience how slums affect the way people feel.
3. You can visit models of the types of houses that Habitat builds in other countries.
4. You can try making bricks the same way as people in some parts of Africa do.
5. The tours of the Global Village motivate people to get actively involved in Habitat.
6. Some people are critical of the village, because they feel the money should be spent on informing people about poverty around the world.

3 How did you decide?

A Group work.   Discuss and report.

1. How did you decide on your profession? Who helped you decide?
2. Did you start out immediately in your dream job?
3. What do you like/dislike about your job?
4. If you could decide again, which career would you choose now? Why?
5. Which careers are more typical for women now and which careers are more typical for men? Why?
6. What jobs do you think might be fascinating, rewarding, difficult or dangerous? Why?

> My first job was in a …

> I think it must be very rewarding to …

> My parents didn't want me to …

> Being a … is probably quite … because …

4 You have the know-how

A Think of some things you know about or can do. They could be things you learned on the job, or in your free time, for example, a sport, a collection you have, a place you have travelled to, a craft you can do, baking or cooking something special, or an organization you know about. Write the three or four subjects on a piece of paper. You are the expert on these topics.

Example:

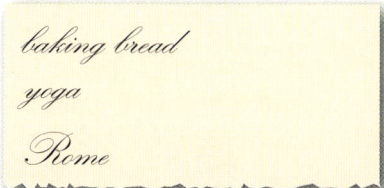

baking bread
yoga
Rome

B Report something you have learned.

12 *Halloween*

1 A spider's web of Halloween words

A Look at file 12 on page 52.

2 Halloween traditions today

A Listen to the interview. Underline the words you hear in the spider.

B Listen again. Correct the statements to make them true.

1. Immigrants brought their Halloween traditions to Europe.
2. Today most children in the US dress up like witches and ghosts.
3. In the US children collect sweets for UNICEF.
4. Teenagers like to eat cold spaghetti.

Did anything surprise you?

> I didn't know that ...

> I'm surprised to hear that ...

> I thought ...

3 Halloween - the history

A **Pairwork.**   True or False? Discuss these statements.

	True	False
1. Halloween is a Celtic tradition that is over 2000 years old.		
2. The Celts didn´t believe in witches and evil spirits.		
3. The Celts wore masks and made big fires to scare away the evil spirits.		
4. The Celts made lanterns out of pumpkins.		
5. Halloween means All Saints' Day.		
6. Trick-or-treating started in England when poor people went from house to house begging for food on All Souls Day.		

B Now read the article and check your answers.

Halloween – The Historical Facts

Halloween has a long history. The end of October is the beginning of winter in Europe. Over 2,000 years ago, people in England, Scotland, Ireland and Northern France honoured Samhain, the Celtic God of death. They thought that at the end of the summer a lot of <u>evil spirits</u>, witches and other evil creatures walked around the earth.

The Celts thought that there was a war going on between the cold, dark winter and the bright sunny long days of summer. They were <u>afraid of</u> things they didn't understand. They were <u>superstitious</u>. So they had ceremonies in order to scare away these evil spirits and protect themselves. At these ceremonies they made big fires and wore masks and animal skins. That's where the tradition of dressing up in costumes on Halloween came from.

The Celts also made lanterns with scary faces out of potatoes and <u>beets</u>. Today we usually make a face in a pumpkin, put a <u>candle</u> in it and put it in front of the house. This is called a jack-o-lantern. Hundreds of years later the Christians celebrated All Saints' Day on November 1st. The evening before was called "All Hallows eve'n". "Hallow" means <u>holy</u> and "eve'n" means evening. That is where the name Halloween comes from.

The tradition of trick-or-treating, going from house to house collecting sweets is old as well. It began on All Souls Day, November 2nd, when poor people went from house to house asking for food. They were given soul cakes, and in return they <u>prayed</u> for the souls of the <u>dead</u>.

---

afraid of: frightened
beet (BE beetroot): a dark red vegetable, that is usually cooked and eaten cold
candle: a stick of wax with a string going through it that you burn to produce light

dead: the opposite of alive
evil spirit: a bad ghost
holy: religious
to pray: to speak to God
superstitious: you believe that certain things are lucky or unlucky

---

4   What do you think?

1. Do you like to dress up and go to costume parties? Why or why not?
2. Did you have a favourite costume when you were a child? What did it look like?
3. Can you name some famous horror films? Why do people like them?
4. What are some common superstitions in your country? (black cats?)
5. What do you think of Halloween celebrations in your country?

People today are not as superstitious as they were in the past, but here are some common English expressions that show that we are still superstitious whether we like it or not.

I have a job interview tomorrow.   *I'll cross my fingers for you.*
This expression is used when we want to wish someone good luck.

I've never had a car accident.   *Touch wood!*
We say this when we want our good luck to continue.

5   The Halloween game

Are you a … ? Is it a … ?   You guessed it.
Now it's your turn.

Your teacher will give you a card.
You can draw it or act it, but no talking, please.

13 *Life long learning*

1 We learn by doing

A **Group work.** Think of three things you learned quickly and three things you have learned through experience. Then read the story.

We Learn by Doing

Not many years ago I began to play the cello. Most people would say that what I am doing is "learning to play" the cello. But these words carry into our minds the strange idea that there exists two very different processes: (1) learning to play the cello; and (2) playing the cello. They <u>imply</u> that I will do the first until I have completed it, at which point I will stop the first process and begin the second. In short, I will go on "learning to play" until I have "learned to play " and then I will begin to play. Of course, this is nonsense. There are not two processes, but one. We learn to do something by doing it. There is no other way.

> **imply:** to suggert sth without saying it directly

B Compare learning an instrument to something you talked about above.

> Learning the cello is like learning to …

2 Circle talk

A Form two circles, one inside the other. Face your partner. Listen to what your teacher says and talk to your partner about it.

3 Hands on Learning: Do-it-yourself tips

A **Pairwork.** Look at the drawings. Can you guess what some of the tips might be? Discuss with your partner.

B Did you guess them all? Now read the article on page 33. Mark the ones you would try.

Hands on Learning: Do-it-yourself tips

1. You must be relaxed to learn. Listen to some music or do something funny. Laughing is very relaxing.

2. Drink water before starting to learn. The brain is less efficient when it is dehydrated.

3. Eat brain food: protein and fruit in the morning, carbohydrates late in the day. Best foods are fish, eggs, nuts, dark green vegetables, chicken and fruit.

4. Make a mind map of what you know and what you would like to learn before starting.

5. Role play. Learn in a different place, wear a costume and use props. This increases memory.

6. Use peppermint or lemon aromas to wake up and help you remember new things.

7. Read a children's book on the topic, rent a video or watch a television programme on the topic. Learn through a different medium.

8. Connect what you know to the new topic and connect what you learn in class to your everyday life.

9. Learn with a friend or in a group. Then teach someone else what you have learned.

10. Remember to keep a positive attitude. Don't worry about how much you learn and how fast. Just keep at it. You will always know more than when you started.

brain: the organ inside your head that controls your thoughts, feelings and movements
dehydrated: not having enough water

memory: your ability to remember
prop: an object used in a film or play

 C Listen to the interview with a learning expert. Which tips does she mention?

D 1. Have you tried any of these things?
2. Would you try any of them?
3. Do the drawnings make you think of any other tips?
4. Look back at the drawings. Can you remember the tips by just looking at the drawings?
5. Do you ever make doodles, little drawings, to help you remember?

4 What do you think?

A Group work. Discuss with your group and report.

1. What is the latest thing you have learned? (how to use a new household machine, a new word, some history or something about everyday life, for example driving to a new place)
2. How did you learn it? (reading, experimentation, watching television …)
3. Do you think you will remember it? Why or why not?
4. Have you ever taught someone to do something? How did you do it?
5. What are the advantages and disadvantages of group work in your opinion?
6. What subjects do you think all children should learn at school?
7. What subjects did / didn't you enjoy at school? Why?
8. Can you remember a good or bad teacher?
9. What makes a good or bad teacher?
10. What kind of things do you learn when you travel?

> I taught …

> I (don't) like group work because …

> I think school children should learn more about …

> I remember my history teacher. She …

14 *Celebrating*

1 Life's little pleasures

A Pairwork.   Have you ever won a prize? What did you win? How did you win it?

B Read the poem. Think of some other things that you could add to the lines in italics?

Little Things

Most of us
Won't win
One of the
Big prizes.
The Nobel.
An Oscar.
The Olympic Gold.
But we can
All enjoy
Life's little
pleasures.

A smile.
Fall leaves
A kiss
The sound
of the ocean.
A full moon.
A parking place .
A log fire.
Friends.
A great meal.
A beautiful sunset.
Cold beer.

Don't worry
About the
Big prizes.
Enjoy the
Small joys.
There are lots
Of them.
Enough for
Everyone.

C Read your poem to the others.

2 Harvest festivals

A Group work.   Each of you will read one of the four files 2, 10, 20, 21 on pages 48, 51, 55, 56 out loud to the others. You will be reading about four different types of harvest festivals in four different countries. Listen to the text and decide where each festival might be.

- Australia
- Canada
- South India
- Ghana and Nigeria

It could be … because they …

I think it's … because …

… was mentioned, so it might be …

B Group work.   Discuss with your group and report.

1. What crops are grown in your area? When are they harvested? Is there a festival then?
2. Is there a special food that your area is known for? Is there a celebration for it?
3. Are the festivals that you read about similar to any of your festivals?

We have lots of … in this area.

We celebrate …

This area is known for its …

3 American Thanksgiving

A True or False?

                                                                                           True   False

1. Thanksgiving in the US is a religious holiday.
2. It is celebrated by almost everyone.
3. It is always on the last Thursday of November.
4. Squanto was a Wampanoag Indian who spoke English.
5. The Indians showed the settlers how to harvest maple syrup and plant corn.
6. Captain Miles Standish asked Squanto to help at a thanksgiving feast.
7. The Pilgrims didn't have enough food so the Indians brought deer, turkey and corn.
8. This first Thanksgiving was a celebration of friendship and peace.
9. Now Thanksgiving is celebrated with only family members.
10. Thanksgiving was not a national holiday until 1863.

B Now listen to the discussion and check your answers.

C Rewrite the false statements to make them true.

D Pairwork. Write down as many words as you can remember from the text. Compare your words with your partner.

E Exchange lists and listen to the interview again. Check the words as you hear them.

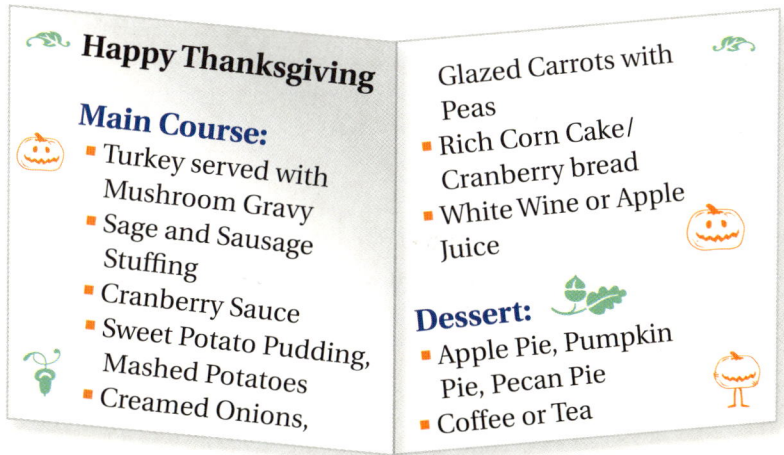

Happy Thanksgiving

Main Course:
- Turkey served with Mushroom Gravy
- Sage and Sausage Stuffing
- Cranberry Sauce
- Sweet Potato Pudding, Mashed Potatoes
- Creamed Onions,

Glazed Carrots with Peas
- Rich Corn Cake/ Cranberry bread
- White Wine or Apple Juice

Dessert:
- Apple Pie, Pumpkin Pie, Pecan Pie
- Coffee or Tea

4 What do you think?

In our family we always …

A Group work. Discuss with your group and report.

I like to invite people over for …

1. Do you have a holiday where special foods are served? What are they?
2. Why are celebrations sometimes stressful?
3. Do you have any special family traditions?
4. Do you like to combine new traditions with old ones? Explain.
5. When do you celebrate with friends, with relatives and with both?
6. What do you enjoy most at celebrations?

There is so much to do – clean …

I enjoy decorating …

15 *Christmas is coming*

1 The Christmas trivia quiz

A Group work.　One pair looks at file 18 on page 55, the other at file 26 on page 58.

2 Christmas in Australia

A Read the e-mail. Underline what is different in your country.

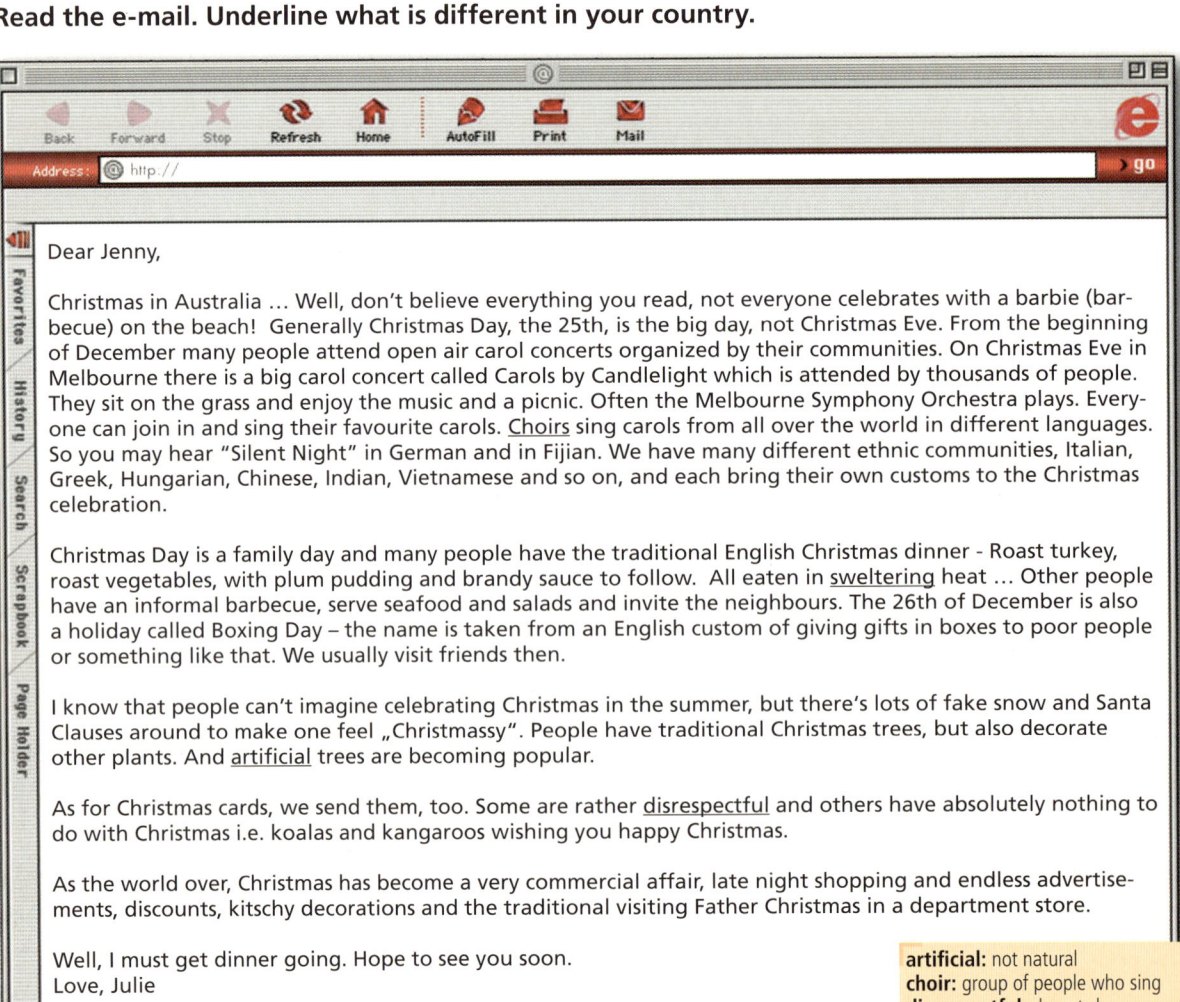

Dear Jenny,

Christmas in Australia … Well, don't believe everything you read, not everyone celebrates with a barbie (barbecue) on the beach!　Generally Christmas Day, the 25th, is the big day, not Christmas Eve. From the beginning of December many people attend open air carol concerts organized by their communities. On Christmas Eve in Melbourne there is a big carol concert called Carols by Candlelight which is attended by thousands of people. They sit on the grass and enjoy the music and a picnic. Often the Melbourne Symphony Orchestra plays. Everyone can join in and sing their favourite carols. <u>Choirs</u> sing carols from all over the world in different languages. So you may hear "Silent Night" in German and in Fijian. We have many different ethnic communities, Italian, Greek, Hungarian, Chinese, Indian, Vietnamese and so on, and each bring their own customs to the Christmas celebration.

Christmas Day is a family day and many people have the traditional English Christmas dinner - Roast turkey, roast vegetables, with plum pudding and brandy sauce to follow.　All eaten in <u>sweltering</u> heat … Other people have an informal barbecue, serve seafood and salads and invite the neighbours. The 26th of December is also a holiday called Boxing Day – the name is taken from an English custom of giving gifts in boxes to poor people or something like that. We usually visit friends then.

I know that people can't imagine celebrating Christmas in the summer, but there's lots of fake snow and Santa Clauses around to make one feel „Christmassy". People have traditional Christmas trees, but also decorate other plants. And <u>artificial</u> trees are becoming popular.

As for Christmas cards, we send them, too. Some are rather <u>disrespectful</u> and others have absolutely nothing to do with Christmas i.e. koalas and kangaroos wishing you happy Christmas.

As the world over, Christmas has become a very commercial affair, late night shopping and endless advertisements, discounts, kitschy decorations and the traditional visiting Father Christmas in a department store.

Well, I must get dinner going. Hope to see you soon.
Love, Julie

> **artificial:** not natural
> **choir:** group of people who sing
> **disrespectful:** do not show respect for the feelings of others, rude
> **sweltering:** very hot

B **Compare the e-mail with Christmas in your country.**

> We don't usually …

> Christmas traditions have changed here, too.
> We used to …

> People here …

> Now more people/fewer people …

---

3 Australian Jingle Bells?

A **Listen and complete.**

1. Some children are _____ of Santa.
2. A Holden is the name of an Australian _____ maker.
3. Ute is short for utility vehicle. This is a pick up _____ farmers use to transport things.
4. An Esky is a container with ice packs you take on a picnic to keep your _____ and drinks cold. Eskimo is the brand name.
5. A kelpie is a sheep _____, a farmer's best friend.
6. You can learn some _____ in Australia.

B **Check file 22 on page 56 for the text of the song.**

---

4 What about you?

A **Group work.** **Discuss with your group and report.**

1. How and when do you decorate your tree?
2. What do you usually have for Christmas dinner?
3. Do you send Christmas cards? How many and to whom?
4. Have you ever spent Christmas in another country? How was it different?
5. Do you remember a special present you received as a child?
6. Why is Christmas sometimes stressful? What can you do about it?

 Christmas Crackers are opened with a bang at Christmas dinner. They contain a crown, a charm and a joke. You can make them yourself or buy them.

> *What did the monkey sing at Christmas?*
> *Jungle bells, jungle bells …*

> *How do you get into a reindeer's house?*
> *Ring the "deer" bell.*

> *A Christmas thought: "Stressed" is just "desserts" spelled backwards.*

> *What did the big candle say to the little candle?*
> *I'm going out tonight.*

16 The New Year

1 A New Year – a new start?

A **Group work.** **Discuss.**

1. What did you do on New Year's Eve?
2. Why do people make New Year's resolutions?
3. Did you make a last New Year resolution? Why or why not?
4. Did you give or receive a special present last year?
5. Are you looking forward to something special this coming year?

I gave my …

I'm planning to …

I've decided to … this year.

I'd like to try to … this year.

B **Report something you talked about.**

2 Good trend or not?

MARK LEWIS

With all the congestion these days, I'm seriously considering buying a car, you know.

A Listen to some people talking about what they would like to see more or less of in the new year. Mark the things they mention.

<u>organic</u> food	understanding
reality TV	violence
fitness <u>fads</u>	crazy diets
chain restaurants	taxes
traffic	new <u>gadgets</u>

fad: sth that is fashionable for a short period of time
gadget: a small piece of equipment
organic: not using chemicals when growing plants or keeping animals

B Complete the sentences below.

I'd like to see more …	I'd like to see fewer/less …

3 New Year – new perspectives?

A Read and underline five words you could use in a discussion.

B Choose three of the topics you would like to talk about. Form interest groups.

1.

We need more rest!

We are all suffering from too little sleep. Your brain is most creative when it is relaxing, dozing or sleeping. In our modern society we sleep too little and therefore cannot function as well as we could. Many accidents are caused by lack of sleep.

2.

Lonely?

Make new friends by using social networking services on the internet. This is a great way to connect with people who are like-minded, for business or pleasure. Have you tried it already or do you know someone who has?

3.

Supermarkets are great, or are they?

They have changed not just our way of eating, but also our cities, the countryside and the economy. We can buy all sorts of exotic foods all the year round. Small shops are going out of business. Most shopping areas are outside of town now and everyone needs a car. What are our alternatives?

4.

Starting a new career?

That means you are open to new ideas, learning new skills and you are enthusiastic. Formal education is becoming less important. What counts is what you can do and what you are willing to learn. People are educating themselves and using their new knowledge. Your hobby could become the basis for your new job.

5.

Kidult = kid + adult?

The 21st century could be the age of the kidult. It is becoming harder to define age groups. On the one hand, children are forced to grow up quickly, and on the other hand, the average computer game consumer is 29 years old. When is middle age and what is old? With people living longer, we have to learn to think in different categories.

6.

The new technologies

are creating a new world where the rules haven't been written yet. What are the restrictions on using camera phones, for example? Can anyone take them anywhere and use them?

7.

Are you a helicopter parent –

one who hovers over your children constantly? It is hard not to be the over-protective parent. After all, it is a cruel, competitive world out there. And who it to blame if the child has problems? The parents. Do we need to protect our children from society or is this over-protection bad for them?

8.

The wellness polarization.

There is an increasing divide between those who are health and fitness freaks and those who are junk food-eating couch potatoes. There are more wellness and fitness trends than we can count. We are bombarded with anti-aging pills and products. Should we fight age or give in? Is there a happy medium? And should people pay more if they don't lead a healthy life?

> **average:** the usual or typical
> **competitive:** wanting to win or be more successful than others
> **cruel:** extremely unkind
> **suffering:** to experience pain or unpleasantness

---

4 ## Auld Lang Syne

Robert Burns (1759 – 1796) is Scotland's best-loved poet. "Auld Lang Syne" is one of his most popular songs and it is traditionally sung on New Year's Eve throughout the English-speaking world. Burns wrote the poem in Scottish dialect and the title means "old long since" or "days gone by". Nowadays people sing modern English versions.

Auld Lang Syne

Should old acquaintance be forgot and never brought to mind?
Should old acquaintance be forgot and the days of auld lang syne?

Chorus: For auld lang syne my dear, for auld lang syne,
We'll take a cup of kindness yet, for auld lang syne.

And here's a hand my trusty friend, give me a hand of thine,
We'll take a cup of kindness yet, for auld lang syne.

17 *High-tech or no tech?*

1 Inventions

Erfinder

Benjamin Franklin, who is well-known as a famous inventor as well as a statesman, was born on January 17, 1706. One of his inventions is the oldest on the list below.

A Group work. List the following inventions in the order they were invented.

B Group work. Which are the seven most useful things in your opinion?
Rank them in the order of usefulness.

3 modern bike
1860 10 contraceptive pills Pille
13 people carrier Minivan
12 Roller Blades inliner
7 Sellotape Tesa
11 seat belt Ausbiralgurt
8 mobile phone/cell phone

6 colour TV
1 bifocal glasses Brille
9 Velcro 1948 Klettverschluss
4 zipper Reißverschluss
14 lap top computer
2 electric fan Fan
5 electric razor

CYBER WITH **ROSIE**   BY ROBERT THOMPSON

OH, YOU'RE STILL BUSY. WOULD YOU LIKE A CUP OF COFFEE?

ONE CLICK FOR YES, TWO CLICKS FOR NO?

CLICK CLICK   CLICK CLICK CLICK   CLICK

C Compare your results with other groups.

2 Are you addicted to technology?

A Pairwork. Interview your partner. Find out if you are a technology freak.

1. How many electronic devices do you have on your desk?
   a) None.
   b) Three.
   c) Five.
   d) More than six. (Please name them.)

2. I could go … without using any electronic devices.
   a) Just an hour.
   b) About six hours.
   c) A day.
   d) Forever.

3. How often do you check your e-mails?
   a) Don't have e-mail.
   b) Once every few days.
   c) Once a day.
   d) A few times a day.

4. Do you use electronic devices while doing sports?
   a) Never.
   b) Just for listening to music.
   c) I use special electronic sports equipment.
   d) Yes, I love high-tech sports equipment.

5. How many different electronic devices do you have in your kitchen?
   a) Less than five.
   b) Eight.
   c) Ten.
   d) More than I can count. (Please name them.)

6. How many do you have in your bathroom?
   a) None.
   b) Just a hairdryer.
   c) A hairdryer and an electric toothbrush.
   d) More than two. (Please name them.)

7. How many do you have in your bedroom?
a) None.
b) Just a clock radio.
c) Radio with a CD player and TV.
d) A home entertainment centre and everything else you can imagine. (Please name them.)

8. How often do you multi-task (use more that one device at a time)?
a) Never.
b) Seldom.
c) Often.
d) Always, otherwise I get bored. (Please name them.)

9. How often do you find yourself wired to the internet, the phone and having face-to-face communication?
a) Never.
b) Every once in a while.
c) Once a day.
d) It happens several times a day.

10. Are you "always available"?
a) No, I don't have a mobile phone.
b) No, I turn my phone off when I don't want to be disturbed.
c) Yes. I have to be, because of work or the children.
d) Of course, I love being able to communicate 24/7.

So what kind of person are you?
If you mostly answered **a** you had better take some tech lessons otherwise you may not be able to use your own phone.
If you answered mostly **b** you are a little old-fashioned, but that's fine.
If you answered mostly **c** you are in danger of becoming a technology freak, someone who is easily bored if not fiddling around with at least 2 or 3 different gadgets at one time.
If you answered mainly **d** you are a real techie! Watch out if the electricity goes off. You are in acute danger of dying – of boredom.

3 Beep, beep, beep!

A Listen to some people talking about technology. Who do you identify with most?

B Which person says these things? Write the number of the person in front of the statement.

1. Modern technology enables a person to spend more time with the family at home. 3
2. It is impolite to talk on the phone and use the computer. 1
3. You can drive and answer your phone messages, it is great. 2
4. Doing one thing at a time is boring. 2
5. I don't worry about the children, because they can call me on my mobile anytime. 2
6. Face-to-face communication is not as important as a phone call. 1
7. People never get a break from work, even on holiday. 4
8. Mobile phones can endanger a relationship. 4

C Pairwork.   Do you agree with these statements?

4 What do you think?

> I could(n't) survive without my ...

A Pairwork.   Discuss.

1. If you had to get rid of some of your gadgets, which five could you do without?
2. Which three could you not do without?
3. Write five rules for mobile phone use.
4. How has technology changed your job and life at home?

18 *What's in a name?*

1 Theme for English B

A Imagine you were sitting in an English class and your teacher said:
"Write a page about yourself." What would you write about? Make a list of things.

B Look at file 23 on page 56 and read the poem by Langston Hughes. Did Langston Hughes write about the things on your list? What different things did he write about?

C Have you ever been in a group were you felt different? When?
How were you different? Discuss.

1. The author writes, "I feel and hear and see Harlem and I hear you". He feels influenced by Harlem where he lives. What other things influence him?
2. What does he say about his relationship to his teacher?
3. What is the mood of the poem?

angry	dissatisfied	pleased	thoughtful
bored	honest	resentful	unhappy

4. Do you remember a place that you especially liked? Was it the first place you went to when you left home?
5. Do you remember a person who influenced you, a teacher, a colleague, or a friend?

In the US February is Black History Month. There are many cultural events in schools and in communities highlighting the important part Black Americans have played in the country's history. Langston Hughes is one of them. He was born in Joplin Missouri, in 1902. After high school and a year in Mexico, he spent a year studying at Columbia University, in New York. His first poem was published in a national magazine when he was 19 and his first book of poetry appeared in 1926. He earned a B.A. degree at Lincoln University in Pennsylvania in 1929. He devoted his life to writing and lecturing until he died in 1967.

2 Which word to use?

In the poem "Theme for <u>English B</u>" the word "coloured" was used to refer to Blacks or African-Americans. Those are the politically correct terms today. What is politically correct language? It means using language which is not <u>offensive</u> or discriminating to a person or a group of people.

A **Pairwork.** Match the traditional word to the politically correct word. Check file 24 on page 57 for the answers.

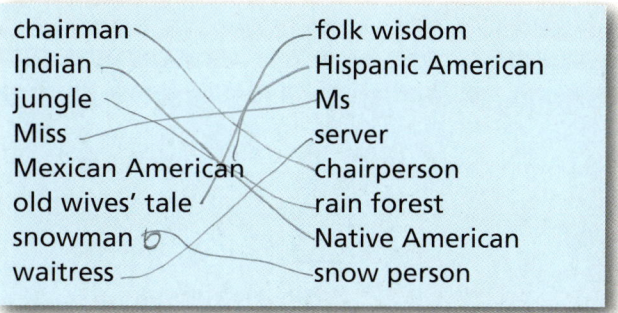

chairman   folk wisdom
Indian   Hispanic American
jungle   Ms
Miss   server
Mexican American chairperson
old wives' tale   rain forest
snowman   Native American
waitress   snow person

B Discuss.

1. What do you think about these "politically correct" alternatives?
2. Can you think of words in your language that have changed?
3. Where do new words in your language come from?

> I don't understand why … is politically incorrect.

> I think that's ridiculous!

> I think language changes the way we think.

> I like using …

C Listen to an interview with a second generation American.

1. What do Maria's parents call themselves?   *mexico,*
2. What does she call herself?
3. What does the interviewer call himself?
4. What do you call yourself?

3 Memory lane vocabulary game

Form two teams.
Choose a name for your team.
One member of each team can keep score. Another member should be the time keeper.
Now quietly write down ten words from previous lessons and give the list to your teacher.
Good Luck!

19 *Valentine's Day*

1 Nice to meet you

A Put your tables in a circle, find a partner and sit opposite each other. You will have four minutes to interview your partner. Start when your teacher gives you the signal.
You may use these questions or make up your own.

1. Where do you live?
2. What are you reading now?
3. What is on your mouse pad?
4. What's your favourite board game?
5. What's your favourite magazine?
6. Favourite smell?
7. Favourite sound?
8. Favourite colour?
9. Favourite holiday destination?
10. Favourite food?
11. Which do you like better – chocolate or chips?
12. Do you believe in telling a white lie to avoid hurting someone's feelings?
13. What was your first car?
14. Storms – are they cool or scary?
15. If you could have any job, what would it be?
16. If you could change something about yourself, what would it be?
17. If you were reincarnated, who or what would you like to come back as?
18. If you had one supernatural power, what would it be?
19. If you could live in another country for a year, where would you like to live?
20. What do you like to do on a day off?

2 Where can I meet Mr or Ms Right?

A Read the questions and then listen to the interview on speed dating.

a) Who invented speed dating? Why?
b) How do you sign up for it?
c) Why do people do it?
d) Can participants expect to get a date after one evening?

We were e-mailing each other every day... Now she considers mine spam.

3 What's your experience?

A Group work.   Discuss.

a) Do you think this is a good way of meeting someone? Why or why not?
b) Do you know anyone who has been successful in finding a partner online?
c) Have you ever tried matchmaking? Was it successful?
d) Where did you meet your partner?

I'd rather …

Yes, in fact, I know someone who …

I met my boyfriend in …

Yes, I invited …

4 Valentine's Day Trivia Quiz

Often valentine cards are humorous and use puns, jokes that you make by using a word that sounds like another or has two meanings. Can you find the puns on the valentine in 4/A? Check your ideas at the bottom of the page.

A Group work. **Read the following statements and decide if they are true or false.**

Valentine's Day Trivia Quiz

1. Valentine's Day probably originated with the ancient Roman feast of Lupercalia which was held on February 15th. One of the customs was that young men could pick a piece of paper with a girl's name on it and she would be his sweetheart for the next year.

2. On February 14th, 270 A.D. Roman Emperor Claudius II beheaded a priest named Valentine for performing marriage ceremonies for so many of his soldiers.

3. During the Middle Ages, people believed that birds chose their mates on St. Valentine's Day.

This led to the idea that boys and girls would do the same.

4. In 1537 St. Valentine's Day was declared an official holiday by Henry the VIII.

5. In the early 1800s valentine cards began to be produced in factories.

6. In Wales, wooden love cups were carved and given as gifts on February 14th.

7. Hallmark, a card company, has over 1200 different cards specifically for Valentine's Day.

8. About 1 billion Valentine's Day cards are exchanged each year. It is the second largest seasonal card sending occasion of the year next to Christmas in the US.

9. Teachers in the US will receive the most Valentine's Day cards, followed by children, mothers, wives and then, sweethearts.

10. Florida produces 60% of American roses.

11. The red rose was the favourite flower of Venus, the Roman goddess of love.

12. About 33% of pet owners

will give Valentine's Day gifts to their pets.

13. Wearing a wedding ring on the fourth finger of the right hand dates back to ancient Egypt, where it was believed that the vein of love ran from this finger directly to the heart.

14. In the United States, 64 percent of men do not make plans in advance for a romantic Valentine's Day with their sweethearts.

believe: to think something is true
carve: to make an object by cutting wood usually with a knife
declare: to announce something officially

Answers: (dear/deer, whale/will, hogs/hugs, bunny/body, purrfect/perfect)

20 *Inspire your heart with art*

1 Art

A What kind of art do you enjoy?

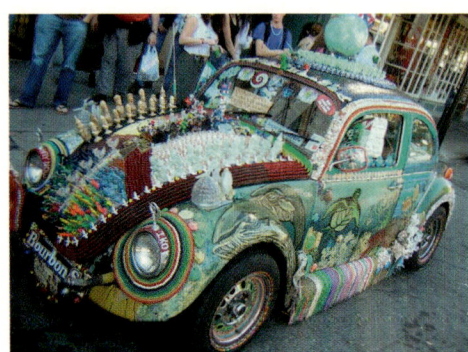

2 Public art

A Listen to three Canadians describe three examples of public art. Write the name of the project under the picture.

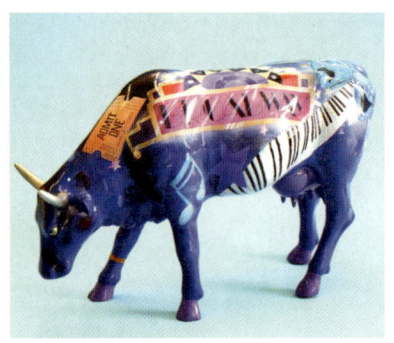

_____

_____

_____

B Listen again and answer the questions.

1. Which project is a big success?
2. Which project was vandalized?
3. Which project is alive?
4. Which is the oldest?

5. Which was sponsored by businesses?
6. Which project changes with the seasons?
7. Which project is temporary?
8. Complete Karl Schutz's motto: "Never let those who say it can't be done, …"

C Group work.   Discuss and report to the class.

1. Which project do you find most interesting? Why?
2. Are there any projects like this in your town or area?
3. Do you think the state should support the arts? Why or why not?

4. Do you have a favourite type of art, artist or work of art?
5. Do you consider these projects art? Why or why not?
6. What is your definition of art?

3   First lines

A   Pairwork.   **Read the first lines of some books. What kind of book do you think it is?**

1   *"By mistake Larry Weller took someone else's tweed jacket instead of his own, and it wasn't till he jammed his hand in the pocket that he knew something was wrong."*

2   *"The first time I saw Brenda she asked me to hold her glasses."*

3   *"He woke up scared.*
Worse than that: he was terrified. His heart was pounding, his breath came in gasps, and his body was taut. It was like a nightmare, except that waking brought no sense of relief. He felt that something dreadful had happened, but he did not know what it was."

4   *"The Englishwoman – her name is Sadie – was fifty-two years old when she decided to leave India. She could hardly believe it. She felt young and free. At fifty-two! Her bag is packed and she is running away."*

5   *"Animals talk to each other, of course. There can be no question about that; but I suppose there are very few people who can understand them."*

4   What happens next? You decide.

A   Group work.   **Choose one of the first lines from 3A. What do you think happens in this book?**

1. Who are the characters? Describe three of them (their looks, their loves and hates and their professions).
2. What do the characters want to achieve in the story? How do they want to do it?
3. What gets in the way of the characters' goals? Are there obstacles, problems or conflicts?
4. How does the main character overcome the obstacles or solve the problems?
5. Do people learn something? Does anyone change?
6. What happens in the end? Is there a happy ending, a tragic ending or is it left open?
7. Which actors would play the main roles in the film of your story?

B   **Tell your story to the others.**

5   What about you?

A   Pairwork.   **Interview your partner. Partner A looks at file 27 on page 58; partner B looks at file 17 on page 54.**

Files

File 1   (0/1A; page 6)

Questions.
1. Hello, my name is …. Where do you live? What about you?
2. What have you got for lunch? What is your favourite food / drink? And yours?
3. What do you like to do in your free time? What sports do you enjoy? What kind of music / books / films do you like?
4. Where do you like to go on holiday? What do you like to do?
5. Where did you go on your last holiday? What did you do? Where did you stay? How was the weather?
6. What do you always take with you on holiday? What do you never take?

File 2   (14/2A; page 34)

In … the Barossa Valley Vintage Festival is held to celebrate the grape harvest. The festival includes wine-tastings, dinners, grape-picking championships, exhibitions of old skills such as barrel-making, choosing a Vintage Queen and a parade. Grapes are harvested from mid-summer until about the end of April. More than half the crop is used for wine-making, while the rest is dried or eaten fresh.

barrel: a wooden container to store wine

File 3   (2/2A; page 10)

Read all about St. Patrick.
When St. Patrick was a young boy he was kidnapped and taken as a slave to Ireland where he was a shepherd. One day while he was praying a voice told him to escape and find a boat that was waiting for him. He ended up in France, where he received some religious training. Later he became a missionary and travelled to Ireland again. There are many legends about St. Patrick. People say that he used shamrocks little green plants with three leaves to explain the idea of the Holy Trinity. From this time the shamrock has been the symbol of Ireland. St Patrick's Day is celebrated on March 17th, the day he died.

File 4   (2/3B; page 11)

Read a story about a leprechaun.
There are many stories about leprechauns. Here is a short one. Once a man from the county of Cork was taking a walk in the forest. By chance he came upon a leprechaun who was sleeping under a tree. He quickly took off his coat, threw it over the leprechaun and caught him. Then he forced the leprechaun to tell him where he kept his pot of gold. Now when a leprechaun is caught, he has to grant the person his wish. He can never refuse. So the leprechaun led the man to a tree. He said: "You will find my gold hidden under this tree." The man marked the tree with a red scarf and went home to get a shovel, so that he could dig up the treasure. Before he left he made the leprechaun promise not to touch the gold or to move it. The leprechaun was true to his word, he left the red scarf tied to the tree, but when the man returned, he found a red scarf tied to every tree in the whole forest. And to this day he is still looking for that one tree. So, when you travel through Ireland, be on the lookout for leprechauns. Listen for the "tic … tac …tic … tac" of the little hammer - and perhaps, under a leaf, you'll find a little man working on a tiny pair of shoes. If you can catch him, you may come back with a lot of gold coins! But be careful, even if you are lucky enough to catch one, he may very well outsmart you in the end.

File 5   (2/4A; page 11)

I'll tell Me Ma

I'll tell me ma when I get (1) _home_
The boys won't leave the girls alone
They pulled my hair and they stole my (2), _comb_
Well that's all right till I get home.

Chorus
She is handsome, she is pretty
She is the belle of Belfast (3) _city_
She is a-courting, one, two, three,
Please won't you tell me who is (4)? _she_

Albert Mooney says he loves her
All the boys are fighting for (5) … _her_
They knock at the door and they ring at the bell
Saying, "Oh my true-love are you (6)? _well_"
Out she comes as white as snow,
Rings on her fingers and bells on her (7) _toes_
Old Johnny Murray says she'll (8) _die_
If she doesn't get the fellow with the roving eye.

Chorus

Let the wind and the rain and the hail blow high,
And the snow come tumbling from the (9) _sky_
She's as sweet as (10) _apple pie_ ,
She'll get her own lad by and by.
When she gets a lad of her (11) _own_
She won't tell her ma when she gets home,
Let them all come as they will,
For it's Albert Mooney she loves (12) _still_ .

File 6   (4/2C; page 14)

Read the interview.
● So what are the official seven natural wonders of the world, Judy?
■ Well, there is an official list - I don't know who thought of it. Anyway, Mt. Everest in the Himalayas is on the list. It is the highest mountain in the world. Then there are the Northern Lights which appear near the Artic Circle. They look almost like fireworks of different hues of blue, violet and pink.
● I've seen them and they are spectacular!
■ Then, there are the overwhelming Victoria Falls in Zimbabwe which can be best seen from the air. The same is true of the Grand Canyon in Arizona. It is the largest canyon in the world and the colours of the stone are magnificent, especially at sunset.
● Yes, they are magnificent.
■ So is the Great Barrier Reef in Australia, which is 2000 km long. It is home to thousands of species of plants and animals. And the corals are some of the most beautiful in the world.
● I've heard that the corals are endangered.
■ Yes, I'm afraid a lot of these places are endangered by pollution and tourists. A relatively new wonder is the Paricutin Volcano in Mexico which was born in 1943. It rose completely unexpectedly in the middle of a field.

- That must have been quite frightening.
- Yes, I read that it certainly was for the farmer who owned the land.
- Was that seven?
- No, the last one is the beautifully shaped Harbour of Rio De Janeiro with its many islands.
- Have you been there?
- Yes, and it is beautiful, but if you ask me, I would say that the world is full of indescribably beautiful natural wonders from the smallest insects to the mighty rivers and the oceans.
- I agree, just look at this place.
- Yes, I think this area here where I work, the Everglades, is a wonder. But nowadays we have to work hard to preserve as much as we can. That's my job here in this park. I try to make people aware of all the wonderful nature around us and the importance of protecting it

File 7   (5/3A; page 17)

Picture (left)
This beautiful sculpture is a tribute to the Right Whale, Georgia's state marine mammal. The young right whales are born in the coastal waters off Georgia and Florida. From December to late March females, calves, and a few males live in this area. This is the only known calving area for Northern Right Whale, which is considered an endangered species.

Picture (middle)
The Waving Girl statue is a popular monument for visitors to the River Street area of Savannah, Georgia. The bronze statue immortalizes a Savannahian named Florence Martus (1869 - 1943), who lived near the entrance to Savannah Harbour and supposedly waved to each ship that came and went - for 44 years!

   The true story is that Florence helped her brother who was the lighthouse keeper on Elba Island at the entrance to the port of Savannah. One day she met a handsome young sailor who was in port and they fell in love. The sailor promised to marry her the next time he came into the harbour. After he sailed she started waving her long apron to greet each ship which entered Savannah's harbour. This went on for years, and in all types of weather. But she never saw the sailor again. To this day sailors report seeing a woman with a long apron and a dog greeting them as they enter the harbour. Is it her ghost?

Picture (right)
The "Behold" statue is situated in Atlanta, Georgia in the Martin Luther King, Jr. National Historic Site in front of the new Ebenezer Baptist Church. It is a tribute to those who like Martin Luther King, Jr. who fought for dignity, social justice and human rights. The sculpture Patrick Morelli was inspired by the ancient African ritual of lifting a newborn child to the heavens and reciting the words, "Behold, the only thing greater than yourself."

File 8   (10/3A; page 27)

Partner B
Tell your partner why you are for the following things. Your partner will have the opposite opinions so think of some arguments for these things. Change partners and go to the next topic when your teacher tells you to change.

I'm for ...
1. Short holidays, a long weekend or at the most a week is enough.
2. Always taking public transport or walking.
3. Travelling around and seeing a lot.
4. Staying at a hotel and eating out.
5. Going to a place I have been before.
6. Going alone.

7. Going to a northern country.
8. Reading a lot about a place before I go.
9. Just buying a few postcards of places I visit.
10. Doing lots of shopping on the trip.
11. Planning my own trip.
12. Going on holiday in the winter.
13. Being prepared for everything that means my suitcases are heavy.
14. Getting up early and seeing as much as possible every day.
15. Staying at home once in a while when you have time off from work.

File 9   (8/1C; page 22)

Kiwis and kiwis
New Zealand's first settlers, the Maori, named the kiwi bird for the sound of its chirp - kiwi, kiwi, kiwi! This flightless bird, about the size of a domestic hen, has an extremely long beak and plumage that is more like hair than feathers. New Zealanders have adopted this nocturnal, flightless and endearing creature as their national emblem. Referring to New Zealanders as Kiwis probably dates back to the First World War, when New Zealand soldiers first acquired this nickname. In the international financial markets, New Zealand's basic currency unit, the New Zealand dollar, is frequently called 'the kiwi'. The dollar coin features a kiwi bird on one side. Perhaps the best-known kiwi is the delicious kiwifruit. Originating in China, kiwifruit were grown in New Zealand's domestic gardens for decades as 'Chinese gooseberries'. However, when enterprising New Zealand farmers began propagating the fruit intensively for export, it was given the name kiwifruit and has since achieved worldwide fame.

File 10   (14/2A; page 34)

Pongal is a popular harvest festival in …. Pongal, which is the name of a sweet rice dish and the festival, starts on January 14 of each year. The celebration lasts for three days. On the first day, Pongal is given to Bhogi or Indran (the rain gods) for providing rain for the harvest. On the second day, pongal is offered to the sun. On the third day, the family's <u>cattle</u> is cleaned and dressed up with flowers, bells, and coloured powder. This is the day to honour the cattle's hard work for helping in the fields. Festivities are different in different regions. Some families clean their houses and throw away old clothes. Neighbours get together for a community feast to share their <u>crops</u> and give thanks to all who have helped at harvest time.

cattle: cows, farm animals; **crops:** plants farmers grow

File 11   (11/2A; page 28)

Group 1

Habitat for Humanity.
Habitat for Humanity International is a non-profit, ecumenical Christian housing ministry. The goal of HFHI is to eliminate poverty housing and homelessness from the world, and to make decent shelter available to all. Habitat invites people from all walks of life to work together in partnership to help build houses with families in need. The houses are built by volunteers, who are the backbone of the organization. They contribute their time for a day, a week, a month or some work on different projects over many years. Individuals, religious organizations and businesses support HFHI by providing tax-deductible donations of money, land and materials that make the work possible. Habitat has built more than 70,000 houses around the world. It has provided 350,000 people in more than 2,000 communities with safe, decent, affordable shelter. The most well-known supporters of Habitat are former President Jimmy Carter and his wife Rosalynn.

File 12 (12/1/A; page 30)

Complete the mind map. Write the words on the spider's legs.

traditions colours costumes animals frightening creatures foods scary sounds

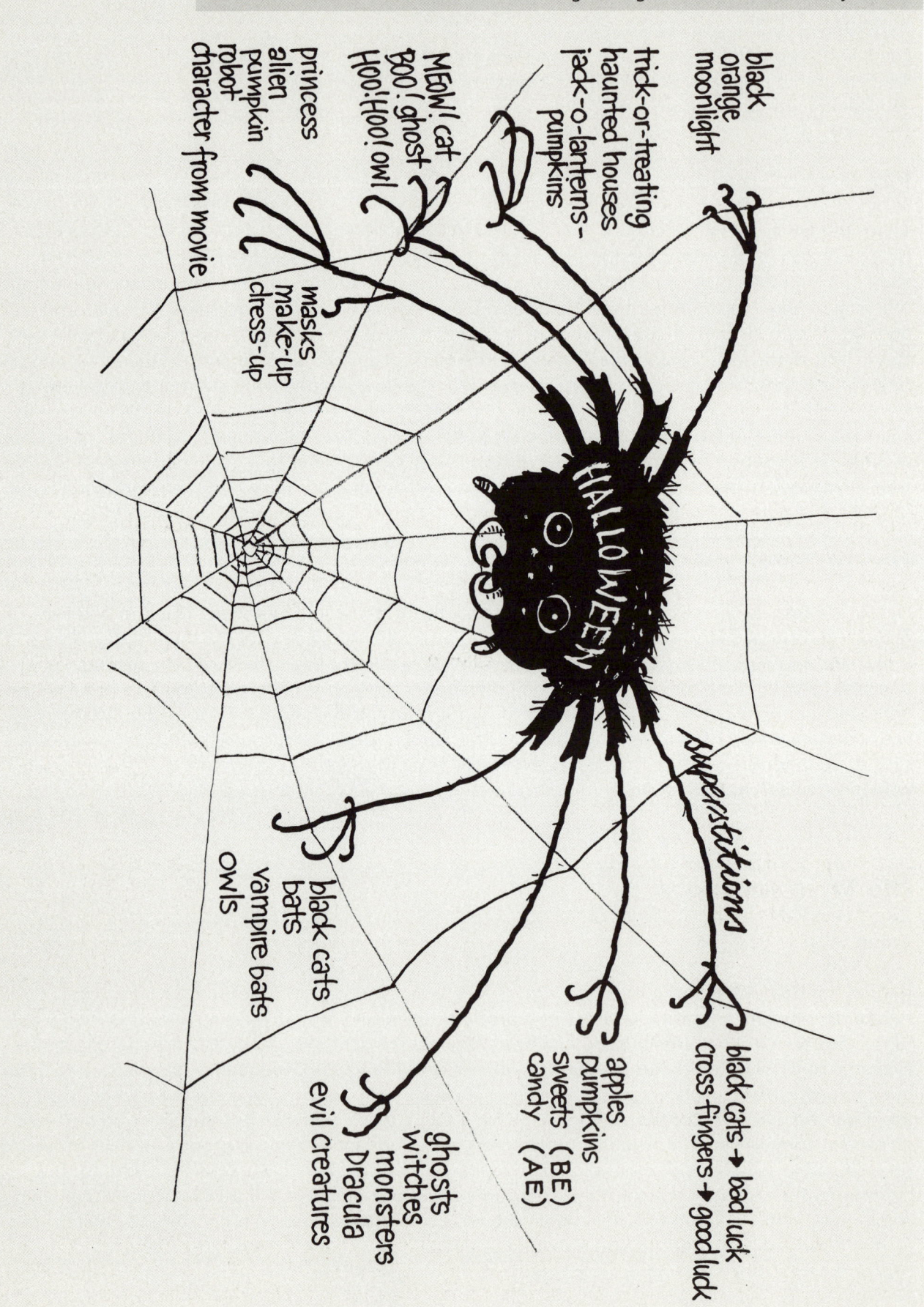

colours
black
orange
moonlight

traditions
trick-or-treating
haunted houses
jack-o-lanterns - pumpkins

scary sounds
MEOW! cat
BOO! ghost
Hoo! Hoo! owl

costumes
princess
alien
pumpkin
robot
character from movie

masks
make-up
dress-up

HALLOWEEN

superstitions
black cats → bad luck
cross fingers → good luck

animals
black cats
bats
vampire bats
owls

foods
apples
pumpkins
sweets (BE)
candy (AE)

frightening creatures
ghosts
witches
monsters
Dracula
evil creatures

File 13 (7/4C; page 21)

Recipes

Couscous with marinated Vegetables

Ingredients
A package of instant couscous with spices
A jar of roasted marinated vegetables
Parsley or basil for decoration

Directions
1. Make the couscous as directed on the package.
2. Cut the marinated vegetables in half.
3. Put a spoonful of couscous on a plate and arrange the vegetables around it.

Chicken Fruit Salad

Ingredients
1 cup low fat raspberry yogurt
1/4 cup mayonnaise
2 tablespoon of honey
4 cups torn butter lettuce
1/2 pound sliced cooked chicken breast, cut into strips
1 cantaloupe, cut into cubes
1 cup raspberries
1 cup blueberries

Directions
Combine yogurt, mayonnaise and honey in small bowl and whisk to blend. Chill. When ready to serve, place lettuce on serving platter. Top with chicken breast and fruit and drizzle with salad dressing.
Tip: You may use other fruits of the season.

Blackberry Shortbread

Ingredients
A package of shortbread cookies
200 grams of marscapone, Italian cheese
250 grams of blackberries

Directions
Spread the short bread with the marscapone.
Mash half the berries and put the berry mixture over the top.
Tip: You may also use stawberries, cherries or peaches.

File 14 (11/2/A; page 28)

Group 2

Building Houses, Building Hope.
Habitat does not build houses for families; rather, it builds alongside those who demonstrate need and willingness to work with Habitat. Homeowner families invest hundreds of hours of their own labour into the houses. Volunteers work with future homeowners to build or renovate houses, which

are then sold to partner families. They have 20 years to pay off their homes with no interest charged. The money goes into a Fund for Humanity which then helps provide the money for the construction of more houses. With this approach Habitat helps partner families regain their dignity that poverty can strip away. When families live in safe decent housing they have more time to spend working towards better jobs, better education and better health. The cycle of poverty is broken, the children will have a better chance in life, the neighbourhoods change for the better and the whole community will improve.

File 15   (10/3A; page 27)

Partner A
Tell your partner why you are for the following things. Your partner will have the opposite opinions so think of some arguments for these things. Change partners and go to the next topic when your teacher tells you to change.

I'm for ...
1. Long holidays three or four weeks.
2. Driving or flying somewhere.
3. Staying in one place and getting to know it well.
4. Camping and cooking for myself.
5. Never going to the same place again, I want to see something new.
6. Going with my family or a group on holiday.
7. Going to a southern country.
8. Making no plans, being spontaneous and discovering new things.
9. Taking a lot of pictures.
10. Wasting no time on going shopping on holiday.
11. Going on an organized tour.
12. Going in the summer.
13. Travelling light, one change of clothes is enough.
14. Catching up on reading and sleeping in as long as I want every day.
15. Always going away someplace when I have time off from work.

File 16   (11/2A; page 28)

Group 3

Millard Fuller, Founder of Habitat.
Millard Fuller was born in Alabama. After college he went to law school where he and a friend began a marketing firm. By the age of 29 he was a millionaire. Although his business was successful, he wasn't happy with his life.

He re-evaluated his life and he and his wife decided to take a big step. They sold all of their things, gave the money to the poor and began to look for a new focus in life. This lead them to Koinonia Farm, a Christian community, where people were looking for practical ways to apply Christ's teachings. There they started several projects to build modest houses on a no-profit, no-interest basis, making homes affordable to families with low incomes. Homeowner families worked building their homes and the homes of others in order to keep the price low and build friendships. In 1973, Fuller moved to Africa with his wife and four children to test the model. The housing project in Zaire, (now the Democratic Republic of Congo), was a success.

File 17   (20/5A; page 47)

Partner B
1. What kind of books do you enjoy reading?
2. Are you reading anything now?
3. Do you have a favourite author? A favourite book?

4. Where do get books ? At the library, buy them, borrow them from friends?
5. Do you think books will be replaced by television, movies, e-books and magazines?
6. How would you define a good book?

File 18 (15/1A; page 36)

Pair A
Christmas Trivia

> **Rules of the game:**
> Read your question to the other group. Give them one minute to answer. Give one point for each correct answer. Give extra points for extra information and two extra points for singing.

1. What do you call the 24th of December? And the 25th ? (2 points)
2. When is Boxing Day and how did it get it's name? (2 points)
3. Name three things that go into plum pudding? (3 points)
4. What kind of Christmas does Bing Crosby want? (1 point)
   Can you sing the song for two extra points? (2 points)
5. What happens if you stand under the mistletoe? (1 point)
6. What is the most famous English Christmas story? (1 point)
7. How many reindeer pull Santa's sleigh? (1 point) Do you know their names? (1 point for each name)
8. What is in a Christmas cracker? (2 points) When is it opened? (1 point)
9. How does Santa arrive to deliver gifts to the children in the Netherlands? (1 point)
10. In which country do children look forward to a piñata at Christmas time? (1 point)

File 19 (11/2A; page 28)

Group 4

Habitat for Humanity Guatemala.
Guatemala is the third largest nation in Central America and approximately 80 percent of Guatemala's population lives in poverty – 50 percent of them in extreme poverty. Housing is a major problem throughout the country. Because of its geographic location, Guatemala is used to natural disasters such as earthquakes, hurricanes, volcano eruptions and floods.

Habitat for Humanity Guatemala was founded in 1979 and has 12 affiliates active in eight states. Current projects include helping families that suffered the loss of their homes due to Hurricane Mitch. HFH Guatemala provides earthquake-resistant houses constructed of concrete floors, block walls and corrugated zinc roofs. A Habitat house in Guatemala typically replaces a temporary structure that lacks a septic system, plumbing or electricity.

HFH Guatemala completed its 10,000th house on Nov. 28, 2001, in El Rosario. It is the new home of Elizeo and Marta dePaz and their three children. The 10,000th house was a part of an 11-house blitz build. Ten of the houses were sponsored by Cisco Systems of the Netherlands and the 11th house, the 10,001th in the country, was sponsored by a couple from California. Volunteers from the U.S. joined young people from 14 countries in Europe and the Middle East to build the houses.

File 20 (14/2A; page 34)

Americans did not invent Thanksgiving, it began in ... Frobisher, an English explorer, and his crew landed in Newfoundland in 1578 and gave thanks for their safe trip to the New World. This was 43 years before the Pilgrims' Thanksgiving in 1621.

Now we celebrate Thanksgiving on the second Monday in October. We have a thanksgiving festival much like the Americans' thanksgiving, but instead of eating turkey, we have ham or lamb and in the country people have *La tourtiere* a pastry pie filled with potatoes and rabbit or pheasant.

File 21 (14/2A; page 34)

The Yam Festival is usually held in the beginning of August at the end of the rainy season. It is a popular holiday in … It is named after the most common food in these countries, yams. Yams are a type of orange sweet potato. People offer yams to gods and ancestors first before giving them to the villagers. This is their way of giving thanks to the gods above them.

File 22 (15/3B; page 37)

Christmas in Australia.
Dashing through the bush, in a rusty Holden Ute,
Kicking up the dust, ESKY in the boot.
Kelpie by my side, singing Christmas songs,
It's summertime and I'm in my T-shirt, shorts and thongs.

Chorus
Oh! Jingle bells, jingle bells, jingle all the way!
Christmas in Australia on a scorching summer's day, Hey!
Jingle bells, jingle bells, Christmas time is beaut,
Oh what fun it is to ride in a rusty Holden Ute.

Chorus

Engine's getting hot, we dodge the kangaroos,
The swaggie climbs aboard, he is welcome too.
All the family's there, sitting by the pool,
Christmas Day the Aussie way, by the barbecue.

Chorus

Come the afternoon, Grandpa has a doze,
The kids and Uncle Bruce, are swimming in their clothes.
The time comes round to go, we take the family snap, pack the car
And all shoot through, before the washing up.

dodge: move quickly to avoid s.o. or sth; **snap:** short for snap shot, photograph;
swaggie: short for swagman. Men who travelled the country in the depression with their possessions in a swag (bag) on their backs.

File 23 (18/1B; page 42)

Theme for English B (Langston Hughes)

The instructor said,

Go home and write
A page tonight.
And let that page come out of you –
Then, it will be true.

I wonder if it's that simple?
I am twenty-two, colored, born in Winston-Salem.
I went to school there, then Durham, then here to the college on the hill above Harlem.
I am the only colored student in my class.
The steps from the hill lead down into Harlem,
Through a park, then I cross St. Nicholas,

Eight Avenue, Seventh, and I come to the <u>Y</u>,
The Harlem Branch Y, where I take the <u>elevator</u>
Up to my room, and write this page:

It's not easy to know what is true for you or me
At twenty-two, my age. But I guess I'm what
I feel and see and hear, Harlem, I hear you:
Hear you, hear me – we two – you, me, talk on this page. (I hear New York, too.) Me – who?

Well, I like to eat, sleep, drink, and be in love.
I like to work, read, learn, and understand life.
I like a pipe for a Christmas present,
Or records – Bessie, bop, or Bach.
I guess being colored doesn't make me not like
the same things other folks like who are other races.   *= race*
So will my page be colored that I write?
Being me, it will not be white.
But it will be
a part of you, <u>instructor</u>.
You are white –
yet a part of me, as I am a part of you.
That's American.
Sometimes perhaps you don't want to be a part of me.
Nor do I often want to be a part of you.
But we are, that's true!
As I learn from you.
I guess you learn from me –
although you're older – and white-
And <u>somewhat</u> more free.

This is my page for English B.

> **elevator (AE):** lift (BE); **English B:** the second English class at college; **instructor:** another word for teacher; **somewhat:** in some ways; **Y:** short for YMCA (Young Men's Christian Association)

File 24   (18/2A; page 43)

Answers.

Native American although politically correct is also thought to be misleading. Anyone born in the US is a native American. So many Indians still call themselves Indians.

Jungle is thought to be old-fashioned. Nowadays people think of the rain forest as a valuable part of our world environment which <u>provides</u> a home for endangered human cultures, plants, wildlife that must be saved for future generations.

Miss is considered sexist. Ms is used to refer to all women.

Hispanic is the popular term today to refer to anyone from Central and South America as well as from some parts of the Caribbean and Spain.

Old wives' tale is <u>considered</u> sexist.

The same is true of snowman.

Waiter and waitress are considered sexist. Server is used for both women and men because it refers to both. The same is true for actress. Many women now refer to themselves as actors.

Steward and stewardess have been replaced by flight attendant.

File 25 (11/2A; page 28)

Group 5

Habitat for Humanity Northern Ireland.
Northern Ireland has gone from an agricultural-based economy to an industrial one. The government has been successful in stimulating economic growth and reducing unemployment rates over the last decade, housing costs continue to increase by an average of 10 percent per year. This makes it difficult for lower wage earners to find affordable housing.

Habitat for Humanity Belfast became the first affiliate in the United Kingdom in 1994. HFH Belfast has a vision of rebuilding houses, communities and hope in an area that has seen 25 years of violence between Catholics and Protestants. In 1997, houses were built in Iris Close, a mainly Catholic West Belfast neighbourhood. More recently, houses were built in Glencairn Estate, a Protestant neighbourhood just across the peace line and near Iris Close. Catholics and Protestants worked on both projects together to help those in need.

HFH Northern Ireland occasionally builds duplexes. Construction is typically done with brick walls and clay tile roofs.

File 26 (15/1A; page 36)

Pair B
Christmas Trivia

Rules of the game:
Read your question to the other group. Give them one minute to answer. Give one point for each correct answer. Give extra points for extra information and two extra points for singing.

1. What is December 31st called? And January 1st? (2 points)
2. What kinds of things do you normally bake before Christmas in Britain ? (1 point)
   In America? (1 point)
3. What are religious Christmas songs called? (1 point)
   Can you sing the first lines to any? (2 points for every Christmas carol)
4. What is the colour of the poinsettia flower?
   (1 point)
5. How many Christmas greetings do you know? (1 point each)
6. Where does Santa live? (1 point)
7. Who do Americans and British people send cards to at Christmas? (1 point)
   What do they do with them? (1 point for each answer.)
8. Which is more important in Japan – Christmas or New Year's Eve?
   (1 point)
9. Which country does the Christmas tree come from? (1 point)
   What do people put on it? (1 point fore each answer – up to 4.)
10. Where is Christmas Island? (1 point)

File 27 (20/5A; page 47)

Partner A
1. What was the last film you saw?
2. What kind of films do you enjoy?
3. Do you have an all time favourite film, actor or actress?
4. If you were making a film, what kind of film would you make? One about everyday life, thriller, a documentary, historical events, love and romance, a crime, a comedy.
5. Do you like to read a book and then see the film?
6. How would you define a good film?

SPECIALITY SHOP

MALL

ANTIQUES

2001 ONLINE

Market

shopping

Good quality

+ It's...
− it's expensive

You can't all things you need at once
+
− it's too big and confusing for me

In summer you can get fresh food
+
−

Open 24 hours every time
+ cheaper
− you can't see the clothes, not very safe

You can discuss many things, things old
+
− to expensive, to...

For old people
try a private ATM or bank
+
− when they don't like things you must go to the post office

Stall − Stand
booth − Stand instead

24/7 round under the...

Mail − order −
katalog

Tapescripts

0 First things first

1A

Hello, everyone. My name is Sandra and I will be your guide on this trip from Munich to Canterbury, England. Our bus driver's name is Chris. Chris is a very careful driver. As you know, Canterbury is in Kent in the southeast of England. It is sometimes called "the garden of England". It is a beautiful sunny day. I hope you are all comfortable. Now before we drive too far I want you to introduce yourself to your neighbour and say a little about yourself.

Well, Chris wants to stop here for a short break. You can get up and stretch your legs and sit down next to someone new.

I see you have all brought your lunches with you. Why don't you tell your new partner what you have brought for lunch and talk about your favourite foods and drinks.

Well, now I know Chris likes Italian red wine. She also wants to stop here for petrol so we will have another break. Get up and stretch your legs and sit down next to someone new.

Now we have just crossed the border and we are in Belgium. Aren't the green rolling hills beautiful? Chris, aren't you driving a little too fast? The road here is not very good. Well, Belgium is famous for its beautiful old historic towns and its wonderful chocolates. Now please introduce yourself and tell your new neighbour where you like to go on holiday and what you like to do.

Here we are at another rest stop. Chris wants to buy some Belgian chocolate before we leave Belgium. So please get up and stretch your legs again. Sit down next to someone new.

Time flies! Here we are on the Belgian coast. I can smell the sea air. There is a warm breeze. No hills or mountains around here. There's a windmill. Aren't the clouds beautiful? We are only about 30 kilometres from the Channel Tunnel. Please introduce yourself and ask your new partner what they like to do in their free time: what sports they do, what kind of music they listen to, what kind of books they like to read and what kind of films they enjoy.

Here we are in Calais at the tunnel. Chris drove so fast, uh and carefully that we are here early, so we'll have a half-hour break. You can do a little shopping, get a snack at the café or restaurant inside or just have a drink. Please stand up and find a new partner. Introduce yourself and ask about their last holiday. Where did they go? What did they do? Where did they stay?

Time to get back on the bus and sit next to a new partner. I know this is probably your first trip with the Eurostar and you are all interested to see what will happen next. Chris will drive the bus into a big train wagon and you can get out if you want. The trip will take about 20 minutes. The Eurostar cost $15 billion and it consists of three tunnels. It is 31 miles long. The three tunnels were built by 13,000 engineers, technicians and workers. Imagine that! Oh, there is the announcement. We are about to enter Britain. Look at the green hills and the sheep. And there is the beautiful blue green sea. There are lots of sailing boats out today. It's a bit windy, but the sky looks friendly. Introduce yourself to your new partner and talk about things you always like to take with you on holiday. Is there something you never take?

Here we are at the hotel. You can go to the reception and get your room key. I hope you enjoyed your trip today.

1 Brand new or second-hand?

2C

In 1948 my parents moved from Portland, Maine to Southern California with their four small children and all their household goods. My mother had some beautiful china. It was her mother's china – a complete set of dishes with hand-painted flowers: forget-me-nots. She packed the whole set of dishes very carefully in four big boxes. The moving company picked up the boxes and drove to California to our new home.

But something happened during the move and one of the boxes never arrived at our new house. So my mother had all the china except for the cups. Every year when we sat down to Thanksgiving or Christmas dinner, my mother would say something about the missing cups.

When my mother died, I got my grandmother's china and on holidays and special occasions we also often talked about the missing cups and where they could be.

One of my hobbies is looking for treasures at antique shops. I also love flea markets. I really enjoy getting to the markets early and watching people unpack their things. One Sunday morning I woke up at 5 am. I don't know why but I immediately decided to go to one of the biggest flea markets in our area, the Pasadena Rose Bowl Flea Market. I jumped out of bed, made a cup of coffee for the road and I drove for about an hour to the Rose Bowl. The sun was just coming up when I arrived. I walked around the outdoor market for a couple of hours.

I was getting tired and thinking of going home when I turned a corner and noticed a table with some china cups. I saw that they were hand-painted – and there were flowers on them. Forget-me-nots! Just like my grandmother's china! I studied the cups carefully. It couldn't be true! These really were my grandmother's missing cups!

The dealer saw how excited I was. She came over to me and I told her the story of the missing box. I asked her where she had found these cups. She said that she had bought a house in the area four years ago and found this box in the attic. When she opened the box and saw the beautiful cups she called the former owner of the house. He said the box didn't belong to him and he had no idea where it had come from. She could keep it. I bought the cups and raced home to tell my family about my miraculous find.

Of course, now when we have a family dinner we always tell the story about the mysterious missing box and how I found my grandmother's china cups at the flea market! I'll always wonder what made me get up at 5am on that morning and drive to that special flea market.

2 St. Patrick's Day

3A/B

As a small child brought up in an Irish Catholic family, I knew all about leprechauns. When I was afraid of a storm, my mother explained that the thunder and lightning were just the leprechauns bowling. When all the pins were knocked down, the sky lit up and that loud noise was the pins crashing down. I pictured these little men dressed in green and felt safe. Oh, and I also blamed the leprechauns when I couldn't find something, my shoe or my key or my homework. It was always "the leprechauns must have taken it."

The word leprechaun comes from a Gaelic word meaning small body. A leprechaun stands about two feet tall and looks like a little old man, his face is wrinkled, but his eyes are bright with mischief. And that means trouble. He is a trickster. He wears green clothes, a leather apron, a cocked hat, and shoes with buckles. All leprechauns are men. Maybe that is why they are grumpy.

Leprechauns are little elves who like to play tricks on people. Their main job is to make shoes for the fairies. Since fairies love to dance, their shoes wear out quickly. Leprechauns are also the bankers of the fairy world. They guard pots of gold at the ends of rainbows. And they enjoy drinking beer made from heath, and smoking their pipes.

According to Irish folklore, a leprechaun must give his treasure to anyone who can catch him. The best time to catch a leprechaun is when he has been drinking. When you catch a leprechaun, you must never let him out of sight or he will vanish in an instant. It is said if you catch a leprechaun you can have his pot of gold or three wishes.

4A

I'll tell Me Ma

I'll tell me ma when I get home
The boys won't leave the girls alone
They pulled my hair and they stole my comb,
Well that's alright till I go home.

Chorus
She is handsome, she is pretty
She is the belle of Belfast City
She is a-courting, one, two, three,
Please won't you tell me who is she?

Albert Mooney says he loves her
All the boys are fighting for her
They knock at the door and they ring at the bell
Saying, "Oh my true-love, are you well?"
Out she comes as white as snow,
Rings on her fingers and bells on her toes
Old Johnny Murray says she'll die
If she doesn't get the fellow with the roving eye.

Chorus
She is handsome, she is pretty
She is the belle of Belfast City,
She is a-courting, one, two, three
Please won't you tell me who is she?

Let the wind and the rain and the hail blow high,
And the snow come tumbling from the sky
She's as sweet as apple pie
She'll get her own lad by and by.
When she gets a lad of her own
She won't tell her ma when she gets home,
Let them all come as they will,
For it's Albert Mooney she loves still.

3 The Red Hatters - Mad Hatters?

4C

● Well, John, you'll be retiring in a few years. Are there any dreams that you would like to fulfil when you have the time?
■ When I retire, I've always wanted to drive around the borders of the United States. I want to start here in California and in the early spring drive north up the coast and across the northern states in the summer. I would get to the east coast and come back through the south where it is warm in the fall and winter. I want to visit friends and relatives that I haven't seen for a long time. I'd love to be able to fulfil this dream. The only thing is I don't want to travel alone. I hope I find someone to go with me and share the experience.

● Holly, do you ever think about retirement?
◆ Not really, it seems a long time away. But now that you mention it, when I have that much time on my hands, I'd like to read all the books I've never had time to read. Maybe see all the movies, too. I guess that is unrealistic, because there is always something new. Oh yes, and I'd like to learn Spanish because I've always wanted to go to South America and I would like to be able to understand the people.

- What about you, Pauline? You're retired, aren't you?
- Yes, I retired from nursing two years ago. And I decided to go to university. I'm studying astronomy now. I've always been interested in the stars and in space, but my parents thought it wasn't practical for a girl to study astronomy. They thought I should become a nurse. So now I have the freedom, the money and the time to study astronomy and I'm really enjoying it. I just take a class or two every semester. I don't bother taking the tests, I just go to the lectures and read the books. I'm just doing it for fun now.

- Have you got any plans, Geoffry?
- I've always wanted to do volunteer work. I would like to help out with a program like Habitat for Humanity. They help people with low incomes build houses for themselves. Or maybe I could do something with young people. I think it is important for senior citizens to give something back to society. I want to help others who have not been as lucky as I have. I also want to get out and meet other people and do something positive for the community. I've seen some people become depressed and lonely when they can't go to the office every day. I want to try to keep myself busy.

5 *Memories and monuments*

2A

- Do you know who Sacagawea was?
- I know she was with Lewis and Clark on their expedition to find a northern route across the continent. And I know that she is on the dollar coin, but other than that, I don't know much about her.
- Yes, I didn't know much, either. But I got interested in her when I saw the coin and have been reading a book about her life.
- So what have you found out?
- Well, most of what we know about her life was written in Lewis' diaries. He describes her as very brave and sensible, and she was only a teenager.
- History at school was dry and dead boring. We learned some important dates and the names of a few famous leaders, it was just a collection of facts. I would have been more interested in learning about people like her. I wonder how she became part of the expedition.
- I read that she was born around 1887. She was a member of the Shoshoni tribe who lived in the area which is now the state of Idaho. Her name means Bird Woman. She was kidnapped by an enemy tribe and then sold to a French-Canadian trader. She married him and they joined the Lewis and Clark Expedition together.
- It sounds like she must have had a hard life.
- Yes, but she must have been very adventurous and intelligent. Once she saved a lot of important equipment when a boat overturned while crossing a river. Another time when the expedition was trying to cross the Rockies and they met some Shoshoni Indians. Sacagawea convinced the Shoshonis to give the expedition food and horses so that they could continue their journey.

- And we know all this from Lewis's diaries? They sound interesting.
- Yes, they do, don't they? Although keeping a diary seems old-fashioned to me today. Nowadays, hardly anyone keeps a diary.
- I think you're right. I don't. I don't have time. Now when anyone explores a new place they take a camera team with them. I just saw an amazing film about the exploration of the Antarctic. It was brilliant! All sorts of fantastic ice formations and wildlife. They interviewed the people who had stayed at the station there for a year and who were planning to write a book about their experiences.
- Do you enjoy reading books like that?
- Yes, I do. Last year I read a book about a group of climbers who climbed Mount Everest. It was really fascinating to learn about how they prepared for the climb and it was exciting to read about the unexpected things that happened.
- I'm more interested in my own family's history. I wish I knew more about how my own great-grandmother lived. I'd be interested in knowing what school was like and how long she went to school. I know she worked in a factory, but I never asked her what the working conditions were like then. I don't know if she married for love or how she met my grandfather. Life was so different then.
- I guess it would be interesting for us to ask our parents and grandparents to write down some of their experiences for future generations.

6 *Something old,…*

3B

First wedding

Well, it was really a last minute decision. We had lived together for five years so we knew each other well. We didn't want a big wedding and we didn't have much money to spend on the wedding either. All my friends found wedding planning so stressful. Where to have the reception, where to find a wedding dress, how many bridemaids to have, what kind of flowers to order, which invitations to order? It was all too much for me to worry about. We lived in California then. I come from Scotland, so none of my family were there and neither were any of Steve's family. None of our friends were around either. So, on the 31st of December we just made a spur of the moment decision to get married. We drove over the border to Tijuana in Mexico. We thought there would be less red tape there. We went to the city hall there and found the person who was responsible for marriages. He was very nice and explained everything. Two women who worked in the city hall were our witnesses. It was very quick and informal, we were both wearing jeans. Afterwards we drove back over the border to California and had a picnic on the beach just the two of us with a bottle of champagne. It was romantic and relaxing. You can see in the picture here that we were very happy. Then we went to look for a motel and our car had a flat tire. That was the only bad part of the day.

Second wedding

Both of us had been married before. I was a widow and Bill is divorced. We wanted a big wedding because we each have a big family and lots of friends in town. We wanted a traditional church wedding, but we didn't want it to be too expensive. So we asked my family to help us make the food for the reception and Bill's family to give us the flowers for the church. I had a beautiful long white wedding dress and my two sisters and two new sister-in-laws were bridesmaids. They wore long burgundy-coloured dresses. A friend made them. There were also four best men, Bill's friends and my brothers. The men all wore formal black suits. They rented them. My mother and sisters decorated the church and the hall where we had the reception. The church didn't allow alcohol, so we drank bubbly apple juice instead of champagne. It took a lot of planning, but that was fun and in the end everything was perfect. Some people think it is a waste of money to have a big wedding, but that is what I wanted. I wanted our two families to all be part of it. They really got to know each other that way. The wedding reception was so much fun we stayed till the very end and then we left for our honeymoon.

7 Berry Good

4B

● With us today is the award winning television cook and author of the No-Cook Cook Book, Axel Dent-Prone. Welcome to the afternoon show, Axel.

■ Thank you, Mary. It's a pleasure to be here.

● Axel, I understand you have written a new type of cookbook. Am I correct when I say it is full of recipes that do not require any cooking?

■ Yes, that's right.

● How did you ever come up with that idea?

■ Well, in my experience, cooking is a very dangerous activity. All sorts of thing can go wrong.

● Like what?

■ Well, Mary, I'm sure you agree that the trickiest appliance in the kitchen is the oven. You can overbake your cake, burn the cookies, cook a roast to death or the oven may even explode. Cooking on the top of the stove is even more dangerous. Just think of how often you have been interrupted while cooking and burned something or worse set the whole thing on fire.

● Well, I haven't set the house on fire yet, Axel, but I don't have a lot of time for cooking and I do get distracted. So, what do I need if I want to avoid accidents on the stove?

■ Well, for my recipes you will only need an electric kettle, a microwave for melting butter or chocolate and the fridge. Remember you can buy a lot of pre-cooked foods in the supermarket these days, so why take any risks?

● You've got a point. Right, I'm having friends over next weekend, what can I serve them?

■ For starters, you can serve couscous with marinated vegetables.

● Couscous - isn't that an African dish?

■ Yes, originally it comes from North Africa, but you can buy it here and you just have to add hot water and let it sit for 10 minutes. You buy a jar of marinated vegetables, cut them up and mix them in with the couscous. Season it with some garlic, salt and pepper. Sprinkle some parsley or something green over the top and you're finished.

● That is easy. What's for the main course then?

■ I suggest you impress your friends with a fruity chicken salad. You buy pre-cooked chicken at the supermarket along with the other ingredients - lettuce, a melon, raspberries and blueberries. Then at home you place some lovely green lettuce leaves on a serving platter. Next you arrange the chicken breast, small pieces of cantaloupe, raspberries and blue berries on top of the lettuce leaves. For the dressing, you mix the raspberry yoghurt with the mayonnaise and honey. Put it all in the fridge and just before you serve it, put the dressing over the top of the chicken and fruit.

● Very colourful! It sounds lovely and very easy. Now, what's for dessert?

■ One of my favourites is blackberry shortbread.

● That sounds heavenly!

■ Well, I think so. First, you take two shortbread cookies and you put a big spoonful of marscapone between them and make a sandwich. Then put some more marscapone on the top. Put this in the fridge till you are ready to serve it. Just before serving, put some fresh blackberries and some blackberry juice over the top. You can use other fruits too, cherries, strawberries, peaches, whatever is in season.

● Yummy, it's almost too good to be true. And with all the fresh ingredients, these recipes sound quite healthy.

■ That's right.

● I'm sure my friends will be impressed that I have managed to put together such an attractive, delicious meal. Thank you.

■ It was my pleasure. And good luck.

8 Something special

1A

I have a favourite place - it is a campsite on the Welsh coast in Pembrokeshire. It is very quiet, it was an old farm and now there are just the ferns, the wild flowers and the heather, a few sheep and cows, the rocky coast, the blue sea and the big sky. The sea air is lovely and refreshing. The view is different everyday, depending on the weather. There is a sandy cove you can walk to and there are wild horses living nearby, lots of sea birds and even a seal or two. There is a lovely view of the rocky coast and a few islands nearby - oh and of course, the sunset is spectacular. That is when it's not rainy. Time flies in this place. And the holiday is always over too quickly.

9 And the living is easy

3/B,C,D

Soon after we moved into our house, I noticed that a corner of the mesh had come loose near the floor and that our cat was using it as a kind of cat flap to come in and sleep on an old sofa we kept out there, so I just left it. One night after we had been there about a month, I was reading unusually late when out of the corner of my eye I noticed the cat come in. Only here's the thing. The cat was with me already. I looked again. It was a skunk. Moreover, it was between me and the only means of exit. It headed for the table and I realized it probably came in every night about this time to hoover up any dinner bits that had fallen on the floor. (And there very often are, on account of a little game the children and I play called "Vegetable Olympics" when Mrs Bryson goes off to answer the phone or get more gravy.) Being sprayed by a skunk is absolutely the worst thing that can happen to you that doesn't make you bleed or put you in the hospital. If you smell skunk odour from a distance, it doesn't smell too bad at all. It's rather strangely sweet and arresting – not attractive exactly, but not revolting. Everybody who has ever smelled a skunk from a distance for the first time thinks, "Well, that's not so bad. I don't know what all the fuss is about."

But get close – or worse still get sprayed – and believe me it will be a long, long time before anyone asks you to dance slow and close. The odour is not just strong and disagreeable, but virtually ineradicable. The most effective treatment, apparently, is to scrub yourself with tomato juice, but even with gallons of the stuff the best you can hope is to subdue the odour fractionally. […]

All this went through my mind as I sat agog watching a skunk perhaps six feet away. The skunk spent about 30 seconds snuffling around under the table, then calmly padded out the way it had come. As it left, it turned and gave me a look that said: "I knew you were there the whole time." But it didn't spray me, for which I am grateful even now.

The next day I tacked the mesh back into place, but to show my appreciation I put a handful of dried cat food on the step. And at about midnight the skunk came and ate it. After that, for two summers, I put a little food out regularly and the skunk always came to collect it.

10 *Have you got the travel bug?*

2A

● Everyone is talking about going away on holiday. But first you have to pack. Today we have Patricia Rosalas here to give us some advice on packing light. She should be an expert because she is a freelance travel writer and has been travelling round the world now for 15 years. Pat, is there anywhere you haven't been?

■ Of course, nobody has been everywhere. I haven't spent much time in the area above the Arctic Circle. I do most of my travelling to cities.

● So, what have you learned from all your travelling?

■ Most important in my opinion are lots of plastic bags, you know the see-through ones you can close. Some of them zip close at the top, those are the best. They are handy for all sorts of things – wet bathing suits, toiletries, dirty clothes and souvenirs you may buy.

● Right, lots of plastic bags and what about suitcases?

■ Suitcases don't have to make a fashion statement. They should be sturdy, but not too heavy. That's very important – weight. And wheels are great, but test them to be sure they work smoothly.

● That's a good point. Some luggage is very heavy.

■ And you don't want to stuff the suitcase with unnecessary things. Take the absolute essentials with you like medicine and an extra pair of glasses. People in other countries use soap and shampoo too, so you don't have to take a large supply.

● What about clothes?

■ First of all, lower your fashion expectations. No one will mistake you for a native of Paris anyway. Coordinate your travel wardrobe. Decide on one or two colours. Layering is the key.

● And shoes?

■ Wear your heaviest shoes. It is easier than carrying them. And while we are on the subject, you can take two pairs. No more. No less. They just weigh you down.

● Are you a roller or a folder?

■ Some people fold clothes. Other people roll them. If you roll, you'll fit more things in and they'll be less wrinkled. I'm a roller.

● So am I. Any additional tips?

■ Yes, don't take anything you will mind losing. Like a favourite pair of diamond earrings or your cherished soap dish. You might leave it somewhere or your suitcase may get lost.

● Yes, I've done that, left my favourite jacket hanging in the closet at the hotel.

■ And I always have an emergency kit with me with some safety pins, a scented candle for smelly rooms, a paperback to put me to sleep, some scissors and most important, a corkscrew.

● Yes, you don't want to be running around late at night looking for a corkscrew. Once I tried opening a bottle with a fingernail file. It turned out to be very messy. Well, have you got any final advice for our listeners?

■ I strongly believe that you should never take more than you can carry comfortably. A light load makes a much more enjoyable trip.

● That's right, there is nothing worse than breaking your arm when trying to lift your own suitcase. Well, thanks for sharing your advice with us today, and next week we'll have …

11 *Do-it-Yourself*

2B/C

■ You have a job here at "Habitat for Humanity" Global Village. How long have you been working here?

■ I've been working here for almost six months. I finished school last year and I wasn't sure what I wanted to do, so I decided to volunteer at Habitat for Humanity and I got a job here at the Global Village.

● What exactly is your job?

■ Mainly, I guide tours around the Global Village,

but I also set up tours, work at the information desk and sometimes in the shop.

● What does Habitat for Humanity do?

■ The mission of Habitat for Humanity is to eliminate sub-standard housing world-wide and replace it with simple decent housing.

● You said it is a world-wide organization. Where does Habitat for Humanity build homes?

■ Presently Habitat builds houses in 92 countries throughout the world and we are still expanding. For example, we have projects in South America, Central America, Africa, India, Europe, the United States and Canada.

● When was Habitat founded?

■ Millard Fuller and a group of friends founded the organisation in 1976.

● What exactly do you show people on the tour of the Global Village?

■ I lead them through the different stations in the Global Village. The first section is a re-enactment of poverty housing you will find in South America and in Africa around big cities.

● You mean you have built a slum in the Global Village?

■ That's right. People have heard about these slums and have seen pictures of them, but walking around one really makes people realize how depressing, unhealthy and demoralizing it is for the people who live there 24/7.

● What else do you show them?

■ Then we visit different houses that Habitat builds in the different countries throughout the world. I explain the special features of the houses and I try to bring the culture of the country closer to our visitors, by explaining the economic situation and the living conditions in the country to the group. For example, let's take a look at the Haiti House. Haiti is one of the poorest countries in the world. The island is also hit by terrible hurricanes. The homes there have to be very sturdy. This brick house is completely reinforced with steel, there are no windows, just these special bricks that let enough light through, so that in a hurricane the house will not blow away and there will be no damage to glass windows.

● Has this type of house been tested?

■ Yes, we were proud that none of the Habitat houses were damaged in Hurricane Andrew.

● That's good to hear. So how long is a tour?

■ It really depends on the interests of the group. If they are interested in making a brick the way they are produced in Africa for Habitat houses, then the tour is longer. It ranges from 30 minutes to two hours. Younger people really enjoy the brick making experience.

● How many people do you take on each tour and how much does it cost?

■ The maximum is 30 but I prefer a smaller group. We ask for a donation of $5. for adults and $3 for children, students and senior citizens. We have all kinds of groups visiting here, from pre-school children to college student groups, along with church groups, senior groups and business organizations, besides individual visitors of all ages.

● What kinds of comments do the visitors make?

■ Most visitors are very moved by the idea of the or-
ganization and they are amazed by the different houses in the village and how people live in these countries. Most visitors are enthusiastic about the organization and they are motivated to donate some of their time or money to Habitat.

● So anyone can volunteer?

■ Yes, of course. Everyone can help. And by the way, some people are critical of the village and say that the money for the Global Village & Discovery Center should have been used to build more houses around the world.

● What is your answer to that?

■ We feel that the Global Village will inspire more people to become involved in the project, so it will be an investment that pays off in the end.

● How do people apply for a Habitat house?

■ You fill out an application for a house. Families who are accepted receive an interest free loan that they have 20 years to pay off and they must volunteer for 500 hours and work on a Habitat housing project.

● It sure sounds like a worthwhile project.

■ Yes, it really is. If you want more information look it up on the website. www.habitat.org .

● Thank you for your time. Oh, just one more thing, has this experience helped you decide what you want to do?

■ Not exactly, but I know now that I want to work with people and I don't want a desk job.

● Well, good luck and thank you.

12 *Halloween*

2A/B

■ The history of Halloween is all very interesting, but how did the traditions come to the US?

● Well, of course, the settlers from Britain brought their traditions with them. At first Halloween was not widely celebrated in the US, but after large numbers of Irish and Scottish immigrants came to the States in the 1800s Halloween was celebrated by more and more people.

● So, how is it celebrated today?

■ Well, it depends. Children dress up - they wear all sorts of costumes. For example, princesses, pumpkins, robots and even silly things like palm trees or refrigerators. Cartoon characters or characters from children's movies are popular.

● So they don't just dress up as witches, ghosts and black cats?

■ That's right. It's lots of fun for children to plan what they are going to wear ahead of time.

● Do children still go trick-or-treating?

■ Yes, they do. That is what they really enjoy. Running around in the early evening in the dark, ringing doorbells and collecting candy. It is a little scary, but their parents go with them. Some children collect money for UNICEF in special cartons.

● Isn't trick-or-treating dangerous?

■ Yes, unfortunately. Now in areas where people don't know their neighbours anymore, cities, for example, parents and schools arrange parties for the children instead of going trick-or-treating.

● What about jack-o-lanterns? Do you still see them?

- Oh, yes, people enjoy carving pumpkins and putting them in front of their houses or in windows. Some of them are real works of art.
- What about teenagers and adults?
- Well, they don't go trick-or-treating, only the younger kids do that. But they enjoy costume parties. Teenagers like to watch horror movies together and visit haunted houses.
- Haunted houses, what are they?
- Well, a group of usually young people set up a house with scary scenes, with ghosts, witches and lots of scary noises. There are also horrible things to touch and feel in the dark, like cold spaghetti, peeled grapes, pudding and other horrible things.
- Sounds like fun, if you like that sort of thing.
- Oh believe me, it is. But some people think this sort of celebration is anti-Christian and don't allow their children to celebrate anymore.
- It is interesting how celebrations change over the centuries and traditions travel all over the world.
- Yes, I think TV and films have a lot to do with that.

13 *Life long learning*

3C

- Today we have an expert on "hands-on learning", Mary Clever. She has been studying how the brain learns and remembers things. So I hope she can give us some tips. Could you tell us what "hands on learning" means?
- Sure, let me give you an example. Take building a house. Some people might read a book about it and have some theoretical knowledge. "Hands-on learning" would be to read a book, but also to talk to people, make a plan, buy the materials, build each part of the house, make mistakes and find solutions for the problems. It is a much more intensive learning experience.
- Yes, it sounds like it. Well, I hope you can give us some learning tips.
- Yes, I hope so, too. First of all, our brain learns better when it is relaxed.
- Sounds logical. You can't learn when you are afraid.
- Exactly. So, I like to start my classes with some relaxing exercises, some music or a funny story to help people wind down and get ready to learn. A good laugh is always very relaxing.
- That's right, it is. What kind of music do you play?
- Well, baroque music like Mozart has been proven to increase brain activity, but I think popular music or sing-a-longs are just as good. It is also good to set goals - to think about what you want to learn and what you want to use it for.
- Yes, that's a good point. For example, in an English conversation class your goal might be to be able to talk about politics with English friends on your next trip to England.
- That's right. So the first step is to make a mind map of all the words you already know that might be useful when discussing politics. And go from there. Ask your teacher questions.
- Well, that seems logical, but I have never done it. What about nutrition and vitamin pills? You hear so much today about the pills and herbs you can take which will increase your memory.
- You do, don't you? I believe a healthy diet is more important than magic memory pills. Fish, nuts, fruit, green vegetables are all brain foods. And many people don't realize how important it is to drink water. The brain needs water to function.
- Well, drinking water is easy enough and inexpensive, too.
- Yes, and there are other ways to learn effectively. Using all your senses is important.
- What do you mean? We use our eyes and ears, but taste, touch and smell?
- Yes, exactly. You can use different aromas to wake up your brain. Lemon and peppermint are good energizers. Suck a peppermint or drink some peppermint tea. Prepare a snack and eat it while learning. It could have something to do with what you are learning. Use your imagination and link learning with daily activities.
- So, we should be listening to Mozart, drinking peppermint tea and eating nuts and burning lemon-scented candles while learning new vocabulary.
- Now you are catching on. You can also try learning the subject in another way – by watching a movie, or a documentary on television, reading a children's book, or you can ask someone you know to explain some part of the topic. Or plan a project using some of your knowledge.
- A project?
- Yes, if you are learning Spanish, for example, write a little poem or song in Spanish using what you know. Look for ways to connect what you are trying to learn to your daily life. If you are learning how to use the internet, find an interesting article or a joke, print it out and give it to a friend, better still – email it to a friend.
- I'm beginning to get the idea.
- And a great way to reinforce your learning is to teach it to someone else – or explain a part of it. That's why learning with a friend or in a group is very effective.
- Learning is beginning to sound like fun.
- Yes, learning should be fun and creative. That makes it interesting and you remember more easily.

14 *Celebrating*

3B

- Well, this is my first Thanksgiving in the States, Beth. I'm surprised that it is such an important holiday. Everyone has been making plans for weeks.
- That's right, it is the holiday that is celebrated by most people, because it is not connected to any one religion.
- What do you mean?
- Well, Christmas, for example, is not celebrated by everyone. Thanksgiving is a day when people give thanks in general for the good things in their lives.
- So people don't go to church on Thanksgiving?
- That's right. Thanksgiving is celebrated on a Thursday, the fourth Thursday of November, so for many people it is a four-day weekend. That's unusual for Americans. They use their time off to take a trip to visit friends and relatives.

- Yes, I've heard a lot of people at work talking about going away for Thanksgiving. Anyway, why is Thanksgiving celebrated?
- We like to remember the first Thanksgiving in Plymouth where the Pilgrims and the Native Americans, the Indians, feasted together.
- Yes, I've heard that. Is it true that the Indians helped the colonists to survive the first year?
- Yes, they were lucky to meet a Wampanoag Indian named Squanto who spoke English. He had made friends with an Englishman called John Weymouth and had travelled to England with him.
- The Pilgrims must have been surprised to meet an Indian who spoke English!
- I'm sure they were. Squanto decided to stay with the Pilgrims and help them. He taught them how to hunt for deer and beaver. He also showed them how to grow corn and other new vegetables and how to use fish as fertilizer. He taught them which plants could be used as medicine and which ones were poisonous.
- I've heard that the cranberry was used by the Indians to cure infections.
- That's true, cranberries contain a natural antibiotic. Squanto also showed the settlers how to harvest sap from the maple trees and how to dig clams.
- That's interesting. When was the first thanksgiving then?
- It is difficult to pinpoint the first thanksgiving, in those days the Indian tribes celebrated six thanksgivings a year. One at the beginning of the year when the weather was warm enough for the maple sap to run from the maple trees, the next was the planting feast, then came the strawberry festival, the green corn festival, the harvest feast in late fall, and finally, the end of the year celebration.
- Didn't the Pilgrims also celebrate thanksgiving in Europe?
- Yes, and Captain Miles Standish, the leader of the Pilgrims, invited Squanto and the leaders of the Wampanoag tribes and their families to join them for a thanksgiving celebration. The settlers had no idea that the Indian families were so large and when 90 people arrived for the feast, they did not have enough food.
- So, what happened?
- The tribal leaders gave orders to their men to go home and get more food.
- What did they bring?
- Deer, wild turkeys, fish, beans, squash, corn and berries.
- That's why those are the traditional foods, turkey, corn, cranberries and pumpkin.
- That's right. It was a celebration of friendship and peace between the pilgrims and the Indians, but unfortunately, their peaceful co-existence didn't last long.
- It's sad to think that the people couldn't manage to live together in peace. Was Thanksgiving celebrated from then on?
- No, it only became a national holiday in 1863. That's when Abraham Lincoln decided the American people needed another holiday besides the Fourth of July.

- That's interesting. So what do most people do on Thanksgiving today?
- They have a traditional turkey dinner with friends and family. Usually everyone helps with the meal and brings something. People just enjoy being with their friends and family - talking, playing games, relaxing, watching football on TV or playing themselves and most important, everyone always eats too much.

15 *Christmas is coming*

3/A

- Hello, this is Beth speaking.
- Hi Beth, did you get my e-mail?
- Yes, thanks a million. I was just going to call you and ask you a few more questions.
- OK, fire away.
- You said Christmas was a big party time.
- That's right. It is summertime for us. Beach houses and hotels are booked out months in advance. People really enjoy the break. I know people there can't imagine celebrating Christmas in the summer, but we close the curtains, light the candles and enjoy ourselves. Afterwards we go out and enjoy the beautiful outdoors for the rest of our Christmas holiday.
- Christmas in California is mild, too. You don't really need snow when you have poinsettias growing outside and people decorate their palms. Of course, we have artificial snow.
- We have lots of that artificial snow, too, along with lights and decorations to get us in the Christmas mood. You can visit Santa in every department store. You know, Jamie was afraid of the Santa in our department store last year.
- I don't blame her, she's only four. Anyway, would you like to sit on a strange man's knee and have his scratchy white beard rubbed into your face?
- It depends. Hey, my brother e-mailed me Jingle Bells the Australian way.
- Sing it to me.
- My family has to leave the room. They are tired of my singing. Dashing through the bush in a rusty Holden Ute, Kicking up the dust, Esky in the boot, Kelpie by my side, singing Christmas songs, It's summertime and I am in my T-shirt, shorts and thongs. Oh, jingle bells, jingle bells, jingle all the way. Christmas in Australia on a scorching summer's day, Hey! Oh what fun it is to ride in a rusty Holden Ute.
- That's hilarious, but what is a "Holden Ute"?
- Holden is an Australian car maker and Ute is short for utility vehicle, you know, like a jeep.
- And what is an "Esky".
- That's a cooler - you know you can keep drinks and food cold in it on hot days. Eskimo is the name of the company which makes them, I think.
- And a kelpie must be some kind of animal.
- Yes, it's an Australian sheep dog.
- I think I'm going to have to take Australian English lessons before I go there!
- Don't worry, you won't have any problems. Hey, I've got to go, but I'll sing the whole song for you at our Christmas party. You're coming, aren't you?

- Wouldn't miss it for anything. Thanks again and see you on Friday.
- Bye.

16 *The New Year*

2/A

Text 1
- Excuse me, would you mind if I asked you a couple questions?
- No, go on.
- What would you like to see more of next year?
- The good weather, we had a great summer. I wish it was like that every year.
- And what would you like to see less of?
- Well, I am tired of all those terrible reality TV shows. It really puts you off TV altogether. It seems society is dumbing down, I'd like to see people read more.
- Thank you.
- Not at all.

Text 2
- Excuse me, can I ask you a few questions?
- Yes, but only if they are quick ones.
- What would you like to see more of next year?
- Money spent on education. The condition of some of our school buildings is disgraceful, classes are too large and good teachers should be paid more. We should spend more money on safe places and spaces for young people where they have freedom to be themselves and interact, they need space to try new things out in an informal way.
- And what would you like to see less of?
- Traffic jams, I'd like to see some politician finally make public transport efficient and affordable for all so more people would use it. Anyway, that's why I'm late, sorry I've got to run …

Text 3
- Excuse me, could I ask you a couple of questions?
- Sure.
- What would you like to see more of next year?
- Let me think, I'd personally like more time to spend with my family and friends. It seems like every year I work longer and longer hours. It seems I find less time to play with the kids, go to the gym or just sit down, relax and read a book for a couple of hours.
- And what would you like to see less of?
- Spam, computer viruses, fitness fads, "healthy" junk food, new technological gadgets, and funny-smelling soaps and candles.
- You didn't have to think about that for long.
- No, I didn't, did I?
- Thanks.
- Cheers.

Text 4
- Excuse me, could I ask you a couple of questions?
- OK, if it only takes a minute.
- Sure, what would you like to see less of next year?
- I hate all these chain restaurants and cafés. All the food tastes the same – like plastic. And the factory farming has made vegetables taste like nothing.

- And what would you like to see more of?
- Slow food, you know, home-grown organic vegetables and fruits cooked at home.
- Yes, the slow food movement started in Italy, didn't it?
- That's right, got to go.
- Thanks.
- You're welcome.

Text 5
- Excuse me, could I ask you a couple of questions?
- Go ahead.
- Great, what would you like to see less of next year?
- On a global level - less hate, violence, disease, hunger and poverty.
- And what would you like to see more of?
- I think we should take human rights more seriously and we should take better care of our natural environment.
- Wow, those are serious issues.
- That's right, but these things will all affect our future.
- Right, well, thanks.
- Not at all.

17 *High-tech or no tech?*

3/A

Text 1
I hate it when I am talking to someone on the phone and I can hear the other person working on the computer. I want to have the person's full attention. I also think it is impolite to talk to someone face to face and have them interrupt the conversation because their phone starts beeping. It is even worse when they notice that they have received a text message (beep, beep, beep) and try to read it while talking to me. It makes me feel like everyone else is more important than I am.

Text 2
When I am in a meeting I check my e-mails and send instant messages to colleagues in the meeting. Sometimes I look up background information on the topic of the presentation. I get bored just sitting there listening to one person speaking. I think it is great that I can answer my mail box messages while driving home from work. And on a personal level, the kids can get in touch with me anytime on my mobile, so I don't worry about them as much as I used to.

Text 3
Ten years ago, I had to be in the office 12 hours a day. Now I can spend 9 hours at work and come home and spend more time with my wife and kids. I can help my kids get dressed, have breakfast with them, give them a bath at night and read them bedtime stories and keep in touch with work with my mobile phone and laptop. Of course, the down side is that I am always available now. I can never escape from the office.

Text 4
I hate mobile phones. My girlfriend spends most of the time we are together talking to other people on

her mobile. Either that, or checking and sending text messages. It is really crazy. She sleeps with the thing under her pillow. It is not good for our relationship. I can only get her full attention when I call her on her mobile.

18 *What's in a name?*

- Maria, you said your parents were born in Mexico?
- Yes, they grew up in a small town in central Mexico. They came to the US in 1958 looking for work.
- What kind of work did they find?
- My Dad got a job for a construction company driving a truck and my Mom worked as a cook in a restaurant. But she quit when I was born. There are five children in the family.
- Did you grow up speaking Spanish?
- No, my parents wanted us to speak English because they thought we would do better at school. And we did do well at school and all five of us went to college.
- So, you don't speak Spanish at all.
- Well, it is funny, but I do need to speak Spanish for my job, so I had to take Spanish classes when I was in college.
- Now I warned you that I was going to ask you a strange question.
- Yes, you did. Go ahead.
- There is so much talk about political correctness and there are lots of new words flying about in the media. I just want to know what do you call yourself? Mexican American, Chicana, a Latina, Hispanic, an Hispanic American or none of these?
- There's not an easy answer to that. My parents call themselves Mexican Americans. Everyone of their generation does. When I was in college in the 70s we called ourselves Chicanos – that seemed to be the revolutionary thing to do.
- Were you ever a Latina?
- No, I never thought of calling myself a Latina. I don't know why. That's a newer word the media uses a lot.
- And now?
- Well, now I don't really call myself anything. My kids are Americans, no question about that in their minds. And I am, too, of course. But, I guess I consider myself an Hispanic American. What about you?
- That's a good question. I'm not quite sure. I'm part Indian and part European. I don't like the term Native American, because that means anyone born in the US. If I am anything, I guess I'm a native Californian.
- Yes, I am too.
- Personally, I don't like to label people by their nationality or race. But, obviously, it is useful for business to make marketing decisions and for politicians to make policy decisions.
- And for sociological reasons, too. It is important to understand the difficulties minority groups have in mainstream society.

19 *Valentine's Day*

- As we all know, finding a date has never been easy, unless, of course, you are Julia Roberts or Hugh Grant. But where on earth should Mr or Ms Normal go to meet Mr or Ms Right? Today's generation of singles has not got a lot of time to waste. That's why speed dating is the perfect alternative to barhopping and hoping to find true love. Today we have Shannon Green here in the studio to tell us about a new way you can meet that special person.
- Hello, John. As you said today's singles don't have lots of time to spend finding that special person. And speed dating is a practical way for people to meet and talk to a large number of singles in one evening.
- Where does the idea come from?
- Speed dating was dreamed up by a Los Angeles rabbi in 1999. He realized that single people were finding it difficult to find partners so he created speed dating which he thought was an effective way of introducing singles to one another. The idea was instantly popular after it was featured on a popular TV programme.
- So, how does speed dating work?
- First, you search the internet to find a speed dating event near you and you register on-line.
- Sounds easy enough.
- On the evening of the event an equal number of men and women turn up at the venue, which is usually a nice hotel. People sit at long tables facing one another. Women have a fixed position, the men move one seat along every four minutes.
- Every four minutes? You only have four minutes to decide if the person is right for you?
- Yes, but most people decide even quicker than that in other situations.
- That's frightening, so first impressions are important?
- That seems to be the case. So anyway, after four minutes a foghorn, a bell or something similar sounds and the men have to move on a seat and start again. Every couple has four minutes to talk and decide if they would like to meet that person again.
- You mean, they exchange phone numbers at this point?
- No, everyone gets a sheet of paper with names on it. If they want to meet a person again, they tick the yes box next to the person's name.
- How long are these events?
- The evenings last for three hours and usually you have the opportunity to meet and talk to about 25 different people. Everyone has a chance to mingle in the break and afterwards anyone who feels like it can go to a nearby nightclub.
- It sounds like fun and less embarrassing than the traditional ways of meeting people. But what happens next?
- After the evening is over the organizers inform the participants if any of the people they have

chosen have chosen them. Then it is up to the singles themselves to make a date or not.
- So, now all the people have to do is work up the courage to make a date.
- Yeah, that's the idea.
- You organize these events so you must know if they are successful.
- Yes, in fact, they are very successful. Two thirds of the singles get a proper date from each speed dating event they attend.
- That's a high success rate. It is much better than going out with a group of friends barhopping and hoping to meet the right person.
- Yes, I think that's why these events are popular. In fact, I met my boyfriend one night at a speed dating event.
- Really?
- Yeah, and we've been going out for a year now.
- Great, well, thank you for talking to us today, Shannon. So, listeners out there in radio land, if you are interested in trying speed dating, check out the website at www.speeddating@ …

20 *Inspire your heart with art*

2A/B

Text 1

- First of all, what is public art?
- Well the term public art started to be used in the 1960s. People wanted to get away from the idea that sculpture was the only kind of acceptable "outdoor" art. Cities started to ask artists to create special works of art for specific places.
- That is interesting. So how did the Moose in the City project get started?
- The Moose in the City project was based on Chicago's "Cows on the Loose", a very successful show. It was a great tourist attraction for the city of Chicago. The Mayor of Toronto thought it would be a good idea to copy the idea here. Artists created a herd of 325 moose which were placed all around the city. Each one was unique. Toronto was turned into a grazing area for the moose sculptures.
- Who paid for the project?
- Businesses sponsored it.
- Was it a success?
- Yes and no. Some of the moose were just advertisements for the products their sponsors sell. Others were very original, beautiful and unique. It was interesting to see what the different artists came up with.
- I heard there was some vandalism.
- Yes, there was unfortunately. It was a shame really, that that happened. I personally think there were too many moose around. And it would have been a good idea to get people living near the moose to get more involved in taking care of them. They could have organized little parties for the neighbours when the moose were set up, then people might have identified with the project more and their moose. That might have stopped some of the vandalism.
- That's a good point.

Text 2

- Laurie McGuan is a public artist and her project is a millennium project for the city of Toronto. Laurie, tell us about your project.
- Well, it is called "Circle of Trees – A Time Piece".
- "A Circle of Trees – A Time Piece" You mean like a clock or something?
- Yes, sort of. It is a way of watching time go by. You see, I've planted seven mature maple trees which are about 10 meters high in a circle which is approximately 27 meters in diameter. One of the trees is cast in bronze. The idea is that the bronze tree remains the same while the others live their lives.
- That sounds interesting. So when people look at the group of trees 50 or 100 years from now they can see how time has changed the space here.
- Yes, that's right. There will be a bronze plaque which shows what the area looked like when it was first planted in the year 2000.
- I bet it's beautiful in the fall when the leaves are turning.

Text 3

- Chemainus is a small port on southeastern Vancouver Island. It has a population of approximately 27,000. Today it is known as the world's largest outdoor art gallery. Today we have a member of the original Chemainus Mural Project here to talk with us and give us some background information. So how did this project start, Sandy?
- The person behind the mural project was Karl Schutz. You see, for years the backbone of Chemainus's economy was the forest industry, and then in the early 1980s business began to decline. In 1982, the town council decided to give the tired main street in Chemainus a new look and renovate it. But in 1983, business was so bad that the lumber mill that had been operating for 120 years had to close. Almost 700 people were out of a job.
- I understand the town had only 4000 inhabitants at that time.
- Yes, and when businessman Karl Schutz came up with the idea of painting the history of Chemainus on the walls of the town, many people thought he was crazy. They thought it couldn't be done.
- Now I understand why Chemainus is known as "the little town that did."
- Yes, Karl Schutz was very determined and did not get discouraged easily. So, a committee was set up to plan and co-ordinate the mural project.
- How many murals are there today?
- Today there are 33 murals painted on the walls of downtown businesses.
- What are the paintings like?
- The paintings are of real people who lived in Chemainus and pictures of life in the early years of Chemainus.
- And today 400,000 people visit Chemainus every year to see the world's largest outdoor art gallery.
- That's right. I like to remember Karl Schutz's motto.
- And that is?
- "Never let those who say it can't be done, stand in the way of those who are doing it."
- That's a good one to remember.

Alphabetical Word List

(AE) = amerik. Englisch	(BE) = brit. Englisch	(adj.) = Adjektiv	(adv.) = Adverb

A

acceptable [ək'septəbl] — annehmbar
to acclimate [tʊ'æklɪmeɪt] — akklimatisieren
aches and pains [ˌeɪks n̩ 'peɪnz] — Wehwehchen
to achieve [tʊ ə'tʃiːv] — erreichen
addict ['ædɪkt] — Abhängige(r)
to be addicted to sth [tʊ bɪ ə'dɪktɪd tə ˌsʌmθɪŋ] — von etw. abhängig sein, nach etw. süchtig sein
(in) advance [ɪn əd'vɑːns] — im Voraus
advice [əd'vaɪs] — Rat
to advise s.o. [tʊ əd'vaɪz ˌsʌmwʌn] — jdm. raten
affordable [ə'fɔːdəbl] — erschwinglich
to be afraid of sth [tʊ bɪ ə'freɪd əv ˌsʌmθɪŋ] — vor etw. Angst haben
afterwards ['ɑːftəwədz] — danach
agog [ə'gɒg] — gespannt
agreeably [ə'griːəblɪ] — angenehm
alien (from space) ['eɪlɪən] — Außerirdische(r)
although [ɔːl'ðəʊ] — obwohl, obgleich
to amaze [tʊ ə'meɪz] — erstaunen
to be amazed [tʊ bɪ ə'meɪzd] — erstaunt, verblüfft sein
amazing [ə'meɪzɪŋ] — erstaunlich
ancestor ['ænsestə] — Vorfahre, Vorfahrin
ancient ['eɪnʃnt] — uralt, antik
angry ['æŋgrɪ] — verärgert, wütend
announcement [ə'naʊnsmənt] — Durchsage
to annoy [tʊ ə'nɔɪ] — nerven
to anticipate sth [tʊ æn'tɪsɪpeɪt ˌsʌmθɪŋ] — etw. erwarten
anticipation [ænˌtɪsɪ'peɪʃn] — Erwartung, Vorfreude
to appear [tʊ ə'pɪə] — erscheinen
appearance [ə'pɪərəns] — Erscheinung
appliance [ə'plaɪəns] — Haushaltgerät
to apply for sth [tʊ ə'plaɪ fə ˌsʌmθɪŋ] — beantragen, sich um etw. bewerben
appreciation [əˌpriːʃɪ'eɪʃn] — Dankbarkeit
approach [ə'prəʊtʃ] — Vorstoß
approximately [ə'prɒksɪmətlɪ] — ungefähr
apron ['eɪprən] — Schürze
arresting (striking) [ə'restɪŋ] — faszinierend
artificial [ˌɑːtɪ'fɪʃl] — künstlich
attic ['ætɪk] — Dachboden
available [ə'veɪləbl] — verfügbar
to avoid [tʊ ə'vɔɪd] — vermeiden
award winning [ə'wɔːdˌwɪnɪŋ] — preisgekrönt

B

back and forth [ˌbæk n̩ 'fɔːθ] — hin und her
backwards ['bækwədz] — rückwärts
barhopping ['bɑːˌhɒpɪŋ] — Kneipentour
barrel ['bærl] — Fass
to be based on [tʊ bɪ 'beɪst ɒn] — abgeleitet von
basil ['bæzl] — Basilikum
bat [bæt] — Fledermaus
bean [biːn] — Bohne
beaver ['biːvə] — Biber
beet (AE) [biːt] — rote Beete
to beg [tʊ beg] — betteln

belief [bɪ'liːf] — Glaube
to believe (in) [tʊ bɪ'liːv ɪn] — glauben (an)
besides [bɪ'saɪdz] — außerdem
best man [ˌbest'mæn] — Trauzeuge (des Bräutigams)
bible ['baɪbl] — Bibel
biblical ['bɪblɪkl] — biblisch
bifocal [baɪ'fəʊkl] — Bifokalbrille
billion ['bɪlɪən] — Milliarde
binoculars [bɪ'nɒkjələz] — Fernglas
birds of a feather flock together [ˌbɜːdz əv ə feðə ˌflɒk təgeðə] — Gleich und Gleich gesellt sich gern.
biscuit (BE) ['bɪskɪt] — Keks, Plätzchen
to bite [tʊ baɪt] — beißen
blackberry ['blækbərɪ] — Brombeere
to blame s.o. [tʊ 'bleɪm ˌsʌmwʌn] — jdm. die Schuld geben
to blink [tʊ blɪŋk] — blinzeln
blog [blɒg] — Blog (Internet Tagebuch)
blueberry ['bluːbərɪ] — Heidelbeere
to boil [tʊ bɔɪl] — kochen, sieden
boiling ['bɔɪlɪŋ] — kochend, sehr heiß
bold [bəʊld] — mutig
bone [bəʊn] — Knochen
boo [buː] — huh
boot (BE) [buːt] — Kofferraum
border ['bɔːdə] — Grenze
boredom ['bɔːdəm] — Langweile
to borrow sth (from s.o.) [tʊ 'bɒrəʊ ˌsʌmθɪŋ (frəm ˌsʌmwʌn)] — etw. (von jdm.) leihen
bowling pin ['bəʊlɪŋ ˌpɪn] — Kegel
brain [breɪn] — Gehirn
brand name ['brændˌneɪm] — Markenname
brandy butter ['brændɪˌbʌtə] — Weinbrandbutter (die gewöhnlich zum *Christmas pudding* gegessen wird)
brave [breɪv] — mutig, kühn
bravery ['breɪvərɪ] — Tapferkeit
breeze [briːz] — Brise
brick [brɪk] — Backstein
bride [braɪd] — Braut
bridesmaid ['braɪdzmeɪd] — Brautjungfer
bright [braɪt] — hell
brilliant ['brɪlɪənt] — hervorragend, klasse
bronze [brɒnz] — Bronze
buckle ['bʌkl] — Schnalle
burial ['berɪəl] — Begräbnis
to bury [tʊ 'berɪ] — begraben

C

to cancel [tʊ 'kænsl] — absagen, streichen
cancellation [ˌkænsə'leɪʃn] — Absage, Stornierung
candle ['kændl] — Kerze
candy (AE) ['kændɪ] — Süßigkeiten, Bonbons
careful ['keəfʊl] — vorsichtig
to caress [tʊ kə'res] — streicheln
carriage ['kærɪdʒ] — Kutsche

to carve [tʊ kɑ:v]	schnitzen
to cast [tʊ kɑ:st]	gießen
cat flap ['kæt‚flæp]	Katzentür
to catch on [tʊ kætʃ ˈɒn]	verstehen
cave [keɪv]	Höhle
by chance [baɪ ˈtʃɑ:ns]	zufällig
changeable ['tʃeɪndʒəbl]	veränderlich
charm [tʃɑ:m]	Anhänger, Glücksbringer
cheers [tʃɪəz]	Prost, zum Wohl
cheery (adj.) ['tʃɪərɪ]	fröhlich, lustig
to cherish s.o. / sth [tʊ 'tʃerɪʃ‚sʌmwʌn / ‚sʌmθɪŋ]	jdn. / etw. (wert)schätzen
cherished ['tʃerɪʃt]	(hoch)geschätzt, in Ehren gehalten
childhood ['tʃaɪldhʊd]	Kindheit
china ['tʃaɪnə]	Porzellan
christmas carol ['krɪsməs‚kærəl]	Weihnachtslied
clam [klæm]	Venusmuschel
clay [kleɪ]	Ton
cocked hat [‚kɒkt ˈhæt]	aufgestülpter Hut
co-existence [‚kəʊɪɡˈzɪstəns]	friedliches Miteinander
coin [kɔɪn]	Münze
to collect [tʊ kə'lekt]	(ein)sammeln
collection [kə'lekʃn]	Sammlung
to come up with [tʊ kʌm‚ˈʌp wɪð]	auf etw. kommen
to compare [tʊ kəm'peə]	vergleichen
comparison [kəm'pærɪsən]	Vergleich
competitive [kəm'petɪtɪv]	konkurrierend, es herrscht harte Konkurrenz
cone (ice cream) [kəʊn]	Eistüte
conflict ['kɒnflɪkt]	Konflikt
to be confused [tʊ bɪ kən'fju:zd]	verwirrt, durcheinander sein
congestion [kən'dʒestʃn]	Stau
to connect [tʊ kə'nekt]	verbinden
connection [kə'nekʃn]	Verbindung
conservation [‚kɒnsə'veɪʃn]	Schutz, Erhaltung
conservationist [‚kɒnsə'veɪʃnɪst]	Umweltschützer(in)
to consider sth [tʊ kən'sɪdə‚sʌmθɪŋ]	etw. in Betracht ziehen
considerably [kən'sɪdərəblɪ]	beträchtlich, ziemlich
to consist of [tʊ kən'sɪst‚əv]	bestehen aus
to continue [tʊ kən'tɪnju:]	fortsetzen, weitermachen
contraceptive pill [‚kɒntrə'septɪv ‚pɪl]	Antibabypille
contract ['kɒntrækt]	Vertrag
to contribute [tʊ kən'trɪbju:t]	etw. beisteuern
contribution [‚kɒntrɪ'bju:ʃn]	Beitrag, Spende
to convince [tʊ kən'vɪns]	überzeugen
cookie (AE) ['kʊkɪ]	Keks, Plätzchen
cooler (AE) ['ku:lər]	Kühlbox
corkscrew ['kɔ:kskru:]	Korkenzieher
corn [kɔ:n]	Mais
corn on the cob [‚kɔ:n‚ɒn‚ðə‚ˈkɒb]	Maiskolben
corrugated zinc roof [‚kɒrəgeɪtɪd‚zɪŋk ˈru:f]	gewelltes Zinkdach
costume ['kɒstju:m]	Kostüm
couch potato ['kaʊtʃpə‚teɪtəʊ]	Couchpotato, Fernsehglotzer(in)
courage ['kʌrɪdʒ]	Mut
cove [kəʊv]	Bucht
cow [kaʊ]	Kuh

cranberry ['krænbərɪ]	Preiselbeere
to create sth [tʊ krɪ'eɪt ‚sʌmθɪŋ]	etw. erschaffen, kreieren
cricket ['krɪkɪt]	Grille
crop [krɒp]	Ernte
crowd [kraʊd]	Menschenmenge
crowded ['kraʊdɪd]	gedrängt
crown [kraʊn]	Krone
cruel ['kru:əl]	grausam
cure [kjʊə]	Heilmittel
to cure [tʊ kjʊə]	heilen
curtains ['kɜtənz]	Vorhänge
custom ['kʌstəm]	Brauch, Sitte
cyberspace ['saɪbəspeɪs]	Cyberspace

D

daffodil ['dæfədɪl]	Osterglocke
damaged ['dæmɪdʒd]	beschädigt
dandelion ['dændɪlaɪən]	Löwenzahn
danger ['deɪndʒə]	Gefahr
dangerous ['deɪndʒərəs]	gefährlich
darned chipper [‚dɑ:nd‚'tʃɪpə]	verdammt aufgekratzt, munter
to dash [tʊ dæʃ]	hasten, sausen
date [deɪt]	Rendevous, Verabredung
dead (boring) [‚ded‚'bɔ:rɪŋ]	total, absolut (langweilig)
to deal [tʊ di:l]	handeln
dealer ['di:lə]	Händler
death [deθ]	Tod
decade ['dekeɪd]	Jahrzehnt, Dekade
decent ['di:snt]	anständig, ordentlich
to declare [tʊ dɪ'kleə]	erklären, verkünden
to decline [tʊ dɪ'klaɪn]	fallen, zurückgehen
to decorate [tʊ 'dekəreɪt]	dekorieren
decoration [‚dekə'reɪʃn]	Dekoration
deer [dɪə]	Reh
dehydrated [‚di:haɪ'dreɪt]	ausgetrocknet
demoralizing [dɪ'mɒrəlaɪzɪŋ]	demoralisierend
depressing [dɪ'presɪŋ]	deprimierend
to be determined to do sth [tʊ bɪ dɪ‚tɜmɪnd‚tə 'du: ‚sʌmθɪŋ]	entschlossen sein etw. zu tun
device [dɪ'vaɪs]	Gerät, Apparat
diameter [daɪ'æmɪtə]	Durchmesser
diary ['daɪərɪ]	Tagebuch, Terminkalender
to keep a diary [tʊ ‚ki:p‚ə 'daɪərɪ]	ein Tagebuch führen
to dig up [tʊ dɪg‚'ɪn]	aufgraben
dignity ['dɪgnətɪ]	Würde
disagreeable [‚dɪsə'gri:əbl]	unangenehm
discount ['dɪskaʊnt]	Sonderangebot
to discourage s.o. [tʊ dɪs'kʌrɪdʒ‚sʌmwʌn]	jdn. entmutigen, abraten von
to discriminate [tʊ dɪ'skrɪmɪneɪt]	diskriminieren
disease [dɪ'zi:z]	Krankheit
disgraceful [dɪs'greɪsfʊl]	skandalös
dish [dɪʃ]	Gericht, Teller (AE)
dish(es) [‚'dɪʃɪz]	Teller (AE), Geschirr
disrespectful [‚dɪsrɪ'spektfʊl]	respektlos
dissatisfied [dɪs'sætɪsfaɪd]	unzufrieden
to distract [tʊ dɪ'strækt]	ablenken
distraction [dɪ'strækʃn]	Ablenkung
to disturb s.o. / sth [tʊ dɪ'stɜb‚sʌmwʌn / ‚sʌmθɪŋ]	jdn. / etw. stören
to get divorced [tʊ get‚dɪ'vɔ:st]	geschieden werden

do-it-yourself (DIY) [ˌduːɪtjɔːˈself] [ˌdiːaɪˈwaɪ] — Heimwerken

to donate sth [tʊ dəʊˈneɪt ˌsʌmθɪŋ] — etw. spenden

donation [dəʊˈneɪʃn] — Spende

to make a donation [tʊ ˌmeɪk ə dəʊˈneɪʃn] — eine Schenkung machen

to doodle [tʊ ˈduːdl] — hinkritzeln

doodles [ˈduːdlz] — Kritzelei

down the hatch! [ˌdaʊn ˌðə ˈhætʃ] — runter damit!

downside (upside) [ˈdaʊnsaɪd] — Kehrseite, Schattenseite

to doze [tʊ dəʊz] — dösen

dreadful [ˈdredfʊl] — schrecklich, furchtbar, entsetzlich

to dress up [tʊ dres ˌʌp] — sich verkleiden

to drive s.o. crazy [tʊ ˈdraɪv ˌsʌmwʌn ˈkreɪzɪ] — jdn. zum Wahnsinn treiben

dues [djuːz] — Mitgliedsbeitrag

dull [dʌl] — langweilig

dumbing down [ˌdʌmɪŋ ˈdaʊn] — immer simpler, seichter werden

E

earache [ˈɪəreɪk] — Ohrenschmerzen

earthquake [ˈɜːθkweɪk] — Erdbeben

eccentric [ɪkˈsentrɪk] — exentrisch, unkonventionell

to educate [tʊ ˈedʒʊkeɪt] — bilden

educational [ˌedʒʊˈkeɪʃənl] — lehrreich

elf / elves [elf / elvz] — Elfe(n)

to embarrass s.o. [tʊ ɪmˈbærəs ˌsʌmwʌn] — jdn. in Verlegenheit bringen

embarrassing [ɪmˈbærəsɪŋ] — peinlich

emergency kit [ɪˈmɜdʒənsɪ ˌkɪt] — Verbandskasten, Erste-Hilfe-Koffer

to enable s.o. to do sth [tʊ ɪˈneɪbl ˌsʌmwʌn tə ˈduː ˌsʌmθɪŋ] — jdm. ermöglichen etw. zu tun

to enclose [tʊ ɪnˈkləʊz] — umgeben

to endanger s.o. / sth [tʊ ɪnˈdeɪndʒə ˌsʌmwʌn / ˌsʌmθɪŋ] — jdn. / etw. gefährden

endangered species [ɪnˌdeɪndʒəd ˈspiːʃiːz] — vom Aussterben bedrohte (Tier)art

enemy [ˈenəmɪ] — Feind

to energize s.o. [tʊ ˈenədʒaɪz ˌsʌmwʌn] — jdm. neue Energie (neuen Schwung) geben

equal [ˈiːkwəl] — gleich

to equip [tʊ ɪˈkwɪp] — ausstatten

equipment [ɪˈkwɪpmənt] — Ausstattung

escape [ɪˈskeɪp] — Flucht

to escape [tʊ ɪˈskeɪp] — entfliehen

ethnic [ˈeθnɪk] — ethnisch

evil [ˈiːvl] — böse

to exchange [tʊ ɪksˈtʃeɪndʒ] — austauschen

to exist [tʊ ɪgˈzɪst] — existieren

to expand [tʊ ɪkˈspænd] — vergrößern

expectations [ˌekspekˈteɪʃnz] — Erwartungen

experience [ɪkˈspɪərɪəns] — Erlebnis, Erfahrung

to experiment [tʊ ɪkˈsperɪment] — experimentieren

experimentation [ɪkˌsperɪmenˈteɪʃn] — Ausprobieren, Experimentieren

to explode [tʊ ɪkˈspləʊd] — explodieren

exploration [ˌekspləˈreɪʃn] — Entdeckungsreise

to explore [tʊ ɪkˈsplɔː] — erforschen, untersuchen

explosion [ɪkˈspləʊʒn] — Explosion

expression [ɪkˈspreʃn] — Ausdruck, Wendung

F

fad [fæd] — Modeerscheinung

fairy tale [ˈfeərɪˌteɪl] — Märchen

fake [feɪk] — hier: künstlich (Schnee)

fan [fæn] — Ventilator

fashionable [ˈfæʃnəbl] — modisch

feast [fiːst] — Festmahl

fellow [ˈfeləʊ] — Kerl, Kumpel

fern [fɜːn] — Farn

fertilizer [ˈfɜːtɪlaɪzə] — Düngemittel

to fiddle around with sth [tʊ ˌfɪdl ˌəˈraʊnd wɪð ˌsʌmθɪŋ] — mit etw. herumfummeln, herumspielen

fight [faɪt] — Kampf

to fight [tʊ faɪt] — kämpfen

fingernail file [ˈfɪŋgəneɪlˌfaɪl] — Fingernagelfeile

to fire away [tʊ ˌfaɪər əˈweɪ] — losschießen

firefly [ˈfaɪəflaɪ] — Glühwurm

flat tyre [ˌflætˈtaɪə] — Reifenpanne

flavouring [ˈfleɪvərɪŋ] — Aroma, Geschmacksstoff

foamy [ˈfəʊmɪ] — schaumig

foghorn [ˈfɒghɔːn] — Nebelhorn

to fold [tʊ fəʊld] — falten

fond [fɒnd] — liebevoll

to be fond of sth [tʊ bɪ ˈfɒnd əv ˌsʌmθɪŋ] — etw. gerne mögen

for good [fə ˈgʊd] — für immer

to force [tʊ fɔːs] — zwingen

to force s.o. to do sth [tʊ ˈfɔːs ˌsʌmwʌn tə ˈduː ˌsʌmθɪŋ] — jdn. zwingen etw. zu tun

forget-me-not [fəˈgetmɪnɒts] — Vergissmeinnicht

former [ˈfɔːmə] — frühere, ehemalige

fractionally [ˈfrækʃnəlɪ] — minimal, geringfügig

freak [friːk] — Fanatiker(in)

free-lance [ˈfriːlɑːns] — freiberuflich

to frighten s.o. [tʊ ˈfraɪtn ˌsʌmwʌn] — jdn. erschrecken

frightening [ˈfraɪtnɪŋ] — erschreckend

to fulfil [tʊ fʊlˈfɪl] — erfüllen

fulfilment [fʊlˈfɪlmənt] — Erfüllung

fund-raising (projects) [ˈfʌndˌreɪzɪŋ ˈprɒdʒekts] — Wohltätigkeits(projekte), Spendenaktionen

further (questions) [ˌfɜːðə ˈkwestʃnz] — weitere (Fragen)

fuss [fʌs] — Aufregung

G

gadget [ˈgædʒɪt] — (praktisches) Gerät

garlic [ˈgɑːlɪk] — Knoblauch

to gasp [tʊ gɑːsp] — nach Luft schnappen

to get rid of sth / s.o. [tʊ getˈrɪd əv ˌsʌmθɪŋ / ˌsʌmwʌn] — jdn. / etw. loswerden

ghost [gəʊst] — Geist

ginger [ˈdʒɪndʒə] — Ingwer

glacier [ˈglæsɪə] — Gletscher

glazed [gleɪzd] — glasiert

to go trick-or-treating [tʊ gəʊ ˌtrɪk ɔː ˈtriːtɪŋ] — von Tür zu Tür gehen (an Halloween)

goal [gəʊl] — Ziel

to set goals [tʊ setˈgəʊlz] — Ziele setzen

to grant a wish [tʊ ˌgrɑːnt ə ˈwɪʃ] — einen Wunsch erfüllen

grape [greɪp] — Weintraube

grateful ['greɪtful] dankbar
gravy ['greɪvɪ] Bratensaft, Soße
to graze [tʊ greɪz] grasen, weiden
great-grandmother Urgroßmutter
[ˌgreɪt'grænd,mʌðə]
groceries ['grəʊsərɪz] Lebensmittel
groom [gruːm] Bräutigam
to grow [tʊ grəʊ] wachsen
to grow up [tʊ grəʊ ʌp] erwachsen werden
grown-up(s) ['grəʊnʌp(s)] Erwachsene(r)
grumpy ['grʌmpɪ] mürrisch
to guard [tʊ gɑːd] bewachen
to guess [tʊ ges] raten
gym [dʒɪm] Turnhalle, Fitness Studio

H

habitat ['hæbɪtæt] Lebensraum
hail [heɪl] Hagel
handy ['hændɪ] praktisch
hangover (from drinking) Kater
['hæŋəʊvə]
happy medium goldene Mitte
[ˌhæpɪ'miːdɪəm]
hard [hɑːd] schwierig, mühsam
hardly (adv.) ['hɑːdlɪ] kaum
harp [hɑːp] Harfe
to harvest [tʊ 'hɑːvɪst] ernten
to hate [tʊ heɪt] hassen
haunted house [ˌhɔːntɪd'haʊs] Gespensterhaus
health [helθ] Gesundheit
healthy ['helθɪ] gesund
heath [hiːθ] Heide
heather ['heðə] Erika, Heidekraut
heaven ['hevn] Himmel
heavenly ['hevnlɪ] himmlisch
hedge [hedʒ] Hecke
herbs [hɜːbz] Kräuter
hilarious [hɪ'leərɪəs] urkomisch, zum Brüllen
holden ['həʊldn] australische Automarke
holy ['həʊlɪ] heilig
holy trinity [ˌhəʊlɪ 'trɪnɪtɪ] Dreifaltigkeit
homelessness ['həʊmləsnəs] Obdachlosigkeit
honest ['ɒnɪst] ehrlich
honesty ['ɒnɪstɪ] Ehrlichkeit
honeymoon ['hʌnɪmuːn] Hochzeitsreise, Flitterwochen
honour ['ɒnə] Ehre
to honour [tʊ 'ɒnə] ehren
to hoover up [tʊ 'huːvər ʌp] aufsaugen
to hover over sth über etw. schweben
[tʊ ˌhɒvər 'əʊvə ˌsʌmθɪŋ]
to howl [tʊ haʊl] heulen
hues [hjuːz] Farbe, Schattierung
to hum [tʊ hʌm] summen
human rights [ˌhjuːmən'raɪts] Menschenrechte
humid ['hjuːmɪd] feucht, schwül

I

imagination [ɪˌmædʒɪ'neɪʃn] Vorstellungskraft
to imagine sth sich etw. vorstellen
[tʊ ɪ'madʒɪn ˌsʌmθɪŋ]
to imply [tʊ ɪm'plaɪ] andeuten
impolite [ˌɪmpə'laɪt] unhöflich
to impress s.o. jdn. beeindrucken
[tʊ ɪm'pres ˌsʌmwʌn]

to be impressed [tʊ bɪ ɪm'prest] beeindruckt sein
impression [ɪm'preʃn] Eindruck
indescribably [ˌɪndɪ'skraɪbəblɪ] unbeschreiblich
ineradicable [ˌɪnɪ'rædɪkəbl] unausrottbar, unabänderlich
ingredients [ɪn'griːdɪənts] Zutaten
inhabitant [ɪn'hæbɪtənt] Einwohner(in)
to inherit [tʊ ɪn'herɪt] erben
inheritance [ɪn'herɪtəns] Erbe
inspiration [ˌɪnspə'reɪʃn] Inspiration
to inspire [tʊ ɪn'spaɪə] inspirieren
interest-free [ˌɪntrest'friː] zinslos
to interrupt [tʊ ˌɪntə'rʌpt] unterbrechen
interruption [ˌɪntə'rʌpʃn] Unterbrechung
to invent [tʊ ɪn'vent] erfinden
invention [ɪn'venʃn] Erfindung
inventor [ɪn'ventə] Erfinder(in)
invitation [ˌɪnvɪ'teɪʃn] Einladung
to invite [tʊ ɪn'vaɪt] einladen
issues ['ɪʃuːz] Themen

J

jack-o-lantern Kürbislaterne
[ˌdʒækəʊ'læntən]
to jam in [tʊ dʒæm ɪn] reinstopfen
jam-packed [ˌdʒæm'pækt] proppenvoll
to join in [tʊ dʒɔɪn ɪn] teilnehmen an
joke [dʒəʊk] Witz

K

to keep one's fingers crossed jdm. die Daumen drücken
[tʊ ˌkiːp wʌnz ˌfɪŋgəz ˌkrɒst]
kelpie ['kelpɪ] australischer Hund
kettle ['ketl] Teekessel
to kick up dust Staub aufwirbeln
[tʊ ˌkɪk ʌp 'dʌst]
to kidnap [tʊ 'kɪdnæp] entführen
knowledge ['nɒlɪdʒ] Wissen, Kenntnis

L

to label s.o. [tʊ 'leɪbl ˌsʌmwʌn] jdn. abstempeln
labor ['leɪbə] Arbeit
lack of sth ['læk əv ˌsʌmθɪŋ] Mangel an etw.
lad [læd] Junge
lately ['leɪtlɪ] neulich, kürzlich
lawnmower ['lɔːn,məʊə] Rasenmäher
layer(s) ['leɪə(z)] Schicht(en)
layering ['leɪərɪŋ] übereinanderlegen
to lead [tʊ liːd] leiten, führen
leader ['liːdə] Leiter(in), Führer(in)
leaf, leaves (pl.) [liːf, liːvz] Blatt, Blätter
lettuce ['letɪs] Blattsalat, Kopfsalat
to light up [tʊ laɪt ʌp] beleuchten
like-minded people Gleichgesinnte
['laɪk,maɪndɪd 'piːpl]
to link [tʊ lɪŋk] verbinden
loan [ləʊn] Darlehen, Kredit
(open) log fire ['əʊpn ˌlɒg'faɪə] (offenes) Holzfeuer
long-term, (short-term) langfristig, (kurzfristig)
['lɒŋtɜːm]
(on the) loose [ɒn ðə 'luːs] freiherumlaufen
loose [luːs] locker
to lounge [tʊ laʊndʒ] herumliegen
lox [lɒks] Lachs
luckily ['lʌkɪlɪ] glücklicherweise
lumber mill ['lʌmbəmɪl] Sägewerk

M

to be mad [tʊ bɪ mæd]	verrückt sein
mad as a hatter [ˌmæd ˌəz ə ˈhætə]	einen Dachschaden haben
magic [ˈmædʒɪk]	Magie, Zauber
magnificent [mægˈnɪfɪsənt]	großartig
the main thing [ðə ˈmaɪn θɪŋ]	die Hauptsache
mainstream [ˈmeɪnstriːm]	Hauptrichtung
mammal [ˈmæml]	Säugetier
maple tree [ˈmeɪpl ˌtriː]	Ahorn
marriage ceremony [ˈmærɪdʒ ˌserɪmənɪ]	Trauung, Eheschließung
marriage contract [ˈmærɪdʒ ˌkɒntrækt]	Ehevertrag
matchmaking [ˈmætʃˌmeɪkɪŋ]	Kuppeln
mature [məˈtjʊə]	ausgewachsen, reif
to mean [tʊ miːn]	bedeuten
meaning [ˈmiːnɪŋ]	Bedeutung
medieval [ˌmedɪˈiːvl]	mittelalterlich
to melt [tʊ melt]	schmelzen
member [ˈmembə]	Mitglied
memories [ˈmeməriz]	Erinnerungen
memory [ˈmemərɪ]	Gedächtnis
to mention sth [tʊ ˈmenʃn ˌsʌmθɪŋ]	etw. erwähnen
menu [ˈmenjuː]	Speisekarte
mesh [meʃ]	Drahtgeflecht
to be messy [tʊ bɪ ˈmesɪ]	unordentlich sein
Middle Ages [ˌmɪdl ˈeɪdʒɪz]	das Mittelalter
mighty [ˈmaɪtɪ]	gewaltig
mind [maɪnd]	Geist, Verstand
to mingle [tʊ ˈmɪŋgl]	untereinander vermischen
mischief [ˈmɪstʃɪf]	Unfug, Unsinn
mischievous [ˈmɪstʃɪvəs]	spitzbübisch
mistletoe [ˈmɪsltəʊ]	Mistelzweig
mittens [ˈmɪtnz]	Fäustlinge (Handschuhe)
mobile [ˈməʊbaɪl]	Handy
modest [ˈmɒdɪst]	bescheiden
monkey [ˈmʌŋkɪ]	Affe
monument [ˈmɒnjəmənt]	Denkmal, Mahnmal, Ehrenmal
mood [muːd]	Stimmung
move [muːv]	Umzug
to move [tʊ muːv]	umziehen
mural [mjʊərl]	Wandgemälde
mushroom [ˈmʌʃruːm]	Pilz

N

nightmare [ˈnaɪtmeə]	Albtraum
non-profit [ˌnɒnˈprɒfɪt]	gemeinnützig
nonsense [ˈnɒnsəns]	Unsinn
northwest passage [ˌnɔːθwest ˈpæsɪdʒ]	nordwest Route
to notice [tʊ ˈnəʊtɪs]	bemerken

O

obstacle [ˈɒbstəkl]	Hindernis
obviously [ˈɒbvɪəslɪ]	offensichtlich
occasion [əˈkeɪʒn]	Anlass, Gelegenheit
occasionally [əˈkeɪʒnəlɪ]	ab und zu
odour [ˈəʊdə]	Geruch
offensive [əˈfensɪv]	beleidigend
to offer [tʊ ˈɒfə]	anbieten

old wives' tale [ˌəʊldˈwaɪvzˌteɪlz]	Ammenmärchen
once upon a time (fairy tale) [ˈwʌnsˌəˌpɒnˌəˈtaɪm]	es war einmal …
organic (food) [ɔːˈgænɪk]	aus biologischem Anbau
otherwise [ˈʌðəwaɪz]	sonst, ansonsten, im Übrigen
outfit [ˈaʊtfɪt]	Kleidung
to outsmart s.o. [tʊˌaʊtˈsmaːt ˌsʌmwʌn]	jdn. austricksen
to overbake [tʊˌəʊvəˈbeɪk]	zu lange backen
to overcome [tʊˌəʊvəˈkʌm]	überwinden
to overturn [tʊˌəʊvəˈtɜːn]	umkippen, kentern
overwhelming [ˌəʊvəˈwelmɪŋ]	überwältigend
to own [tʊ əʊn]	besitzen
owner [ˈəʊnə]	Besitzer(in), Eigentümer(in)

P

pace [peɪs]	Schritt, Tempo
to pad [tʊ pæd]	tappen, trotten
park naturalist [ˈpaːk ˌnætʃərəlɪst]	Parkaufseher(in)
parking place [ˈpaːkɪŋ ˌpleɪs]	Parkplatz
parsley [ˈpaːslɪ]	Petersilie
to pass down [tʊ paːsˌdaʊn]	weitergeben
peaceful [ˈpiːsfʊl]	friedlich
to peal [tʊ piːl]	schälen
pecan [ˈpiːkæn]	Pecannuss
people carrier [ˈpiːpl ˌkærɪə]	Minivan
to perform [tʊ pəˈfɔːm]	etw. vorführen, (eine Zeremonie) vollziehen
pet [pet]	Haustier
pheasant [ˈfeznt]	Fasan
pickup [ˈpɪkʌp]	Kleintransporter
pie [paɪ]	Pastete
pilgrim [ˈpɪlgrɪm]	Pilger
to pinpoint sth [tʊ ˈpɪnpɔɪnt ˌsʌmθɪŋ]	etw. genau bestimmen
pipe [paɪp]	Pfeife
plaque [plaːk]	Tafel, (Messing)schild
plate [pleɪt]	Teller
pleasure [ˈpleʒə]	Vergnügen
plumbing [ˈplʌmɪŋ]	Wasserleitungen
poacher [ˈpəʊtʃə]	Wilderer
pod [pɒd]	Hülse
poinsettias [ˌpɔɪnˈsetɪəz]	Weihnachtsstern (Pflanze)
to poison [tʊ ˈpɔɪzn]	vergiften
poisonous [ˈpɔɪznəs]	giftig
policy [ˈpɒləsɪ]	Stratigie, Politik
to pollute [tʊ pəˈluːt]	verschmutzen
pollution [pəˈluːʃn]	Verschmutzung
poor [pɔː]	arm
porch [pɔːtʃ]	Veranda
potluck [ˌpɒtˈlʌk]	Zufallstreffer; Abendessen, zu dem die Gäste verschiedene Gerichte mitbringen und miteinander teilen
to pound [tʊ paʊnd]	klopfen
poverty [ˈpɒvətɪ]	Armut
to pray [tʊ preɪ]	beten
prayer [preə]	Gebet
to become / get pregnant [tʊ bɪkʌm / get ˈpregnənt]	schwanger werden

to prepare [tʊ prɪ'peə]	vorbereiten
to be prepared for sth	auf etw. vorbereitet
[tʊ bɪ prɪ'peəd fə ˌsʌmθɪŋ]	sein
preservation [ˌprezə'veɪʃn]	Erhaltung
to preserve sth	etw. erhalten
[tʊ prɪ'zɜːv ˌsʌmθɪŋ]	
previous ['priːvɪəs]	vorhergehende
promise ['prɒmɪs]	Versprechen
to promise sth	etw. versprechen
[tʊ 'prɒmɪs ˌsʌmθɪŋ]	
proper ['prɒpə]	anständig
props [prɒps]	Requisiten
to protect [tʊ prə'tekt]	schützen
protection [prə'tekʃn]	Schutz
proud [praʊd]	stolz
pun [pʌn]	Wortspiel
pure [pjʊə]	rein
purity ['pjʊərətɪ]	Reinheit
purpose ['pɜːpəs]	Zweck
purse (AE) [pɜːrs]	Handtasche
to put s.o. off	jdn. abschrecken
[tʊ pʊt ˌsʌmwʌn 'ɒf]	

Q

quirky ['kwɜːkɪ]	schrullig
to quit [tʊ kwɪt]	aufgeben

R

Rabbi ['ræbaɪ]	Rabbiner
rabbit ['ræbɪt]	Kaninchen
to raise money [tʊ reɪz ˌmʌnɪ]	Geld auftreiben
raspberry ['rɑːzbərɪ]	Himbeere
razor ['reɪzə]	Rasierapparat, Rasierer
realization [ˌrɪəlaɪ'zeɪʃn]	Erkenntnis
to realize [tʊ 'rɪəlaɪz]	sich klar werden, bewusst werden
reason ['riːzn]	Grund
reception [rɪ'sepʃn]	Empfang
recipe ['resɪpɪ]	Rezept
red tape [ˌred'teɪp]	hier: Bürokratie
re-enactment [ˌriːɪ'næktmənt]	Wiederaufführung
re-evaluate [ˌriːɪ'væljʊeɪt]	etw. wieder schätzen
to refuse sth [tʊ rɪ'fjuːz ˌsʌmθɪŋ]	etw. ablehnen
to regain [tʊ rɪ'geɪn]	wiedergewinnen
to register [tʊ 'redʒɪstə]	sich anmelden
registry office ['redʒɪstrɪ ˌɒfɪs]	Standesamt
reincarnated [ˌriːɪnkɑː'neɪtɪd]	wiedergeboren
reinforced [ˌriːɪn'fɔːst]	verstärkt
relationship [rɪ'leɪʃnʃɪp]	Verhältnis
relative ['relətɪv]	Verwandte(r)
relief [rɪ'liːf]	Erleichterung
reluctantly [rɪ'lʌktəntlɪ]	zögerlich
remedy ['remədɪ]	Heilmittel
to rent [tʊ rent]	mieten
to replace [tʊ rɪ'pleɪs]	ersetzen
replacement [rɪ'pleɪsmənt]	Ersatz
to require [tʊ rɪ'kwaɪə]	brauchen, benötigen
resentful [rɪ'zentfʊl]	verbittert
resolution (New Year) [ˌrezə'luːʃn]	Vorsatz für das neue Jahr
rest [rest]	Ruhepause, Erholung
to retire [tʊ rɪ'taɪə]	in den Ruhestand treten
retirement [rɪ'taɪəmənt]	Ruhestand
to return sth [tʊ rɪ'tɜːn ˌsʌmθɪŋ]	etw. umtauschen
revolting [rɪ'vəʊltɪŋ]	abstoßend, widerlich

ridiculous [rɪ'dɪkjələs]	lächerlich
rocky ['rɒkɪ]	felsig
to rub [tʊ rʌb]	reiben
to ruin [tʊ 'ruːɪn]	zerstören
ruins ['ruːɪnz]	Ruinen
rules [ruːlz]	Regeln
run down [ˌrʌn'daʊn]	heruntergekommen, abgenutzt
rusty ['rʌstɪ]	rostig

S

safety pin ['seɪftɪˌpɪn]	Sicherheitsnadel
sage [seɪdʒ]	Salbei
sap [sæp]	Saft (vom Baum)
to scare [tʊ skeə]	erschrecken
scarf [skɑːf]	Schal
scary (adj.) ['skeərɪ]	Furcht erregend
to (keep) score [tʊ (kiːp) skɔː]	Punkte zählen
scratchy ['skrætʃɪ]	kratzig
screen [skriːn]	Fliegengitter
screened [skriːnd]	mit Fliegengitter ausgestattet
to scrub [tʊ skrʌb]	schrubben
seafood ['siːfuːd]	Meeresfrüchte
see-through ['siːθruː]	durchsichtig
Sellotape ['seləteɪp]	Tesafilm
separately ['seprətlɪ]	separat, getrennt
septic system ['septɪk ˌsɪstəm]	Klärsystem
settler ['setlə]	Siedler(in)
shape [ʃeɪp]	Form
shaped [ʃeɪpt]	geformt
sheep [ʃiːp]	Schaf
sheet [ʃiːt]	Blatt (Papier)
shells [ʃelz]	Muscheln
shelter ['ʃeltə]	Unterkunft
shepherd ['ʃepəd]	Schäfer
to shop till you drop [tʊ ˌʃɒp tɪl jʊ 'drɒp]	einkaufen bis zum Umfallen
shovel ['ʃʌvl]	Spaten
to sign up [tʊ saɪnˌʌp]	sich anmelden
similar ['sɪmɪlə]	ähnlich
skills [skɪlz]	Fertigkeiten, Fähigkeiten
skin [skɪn]	Haut
skunk [skʌŋk]	Stinktier
slave [sleɪv]	Sklave, Sklavin
sleigh [sleɪ]	Schlitten
to slice sth [tʊ 'slaɪsˌsʌmθɪŋ]	etw. in Scheiben schneiden
sliced [slaɪst]	in Scheiben geschnitten
smoothly ['smuːðlɪ]	reibungslos
snort [snɔːt]	schnaufen
soldier ['səʊldʒə]	Soldat(in)
spam [spæm]	ungewollte E-Mail
special occasion [ˌspeʃl ə'keɪʒn]	besondere Gelegenheit
spectacular [spek'tækjələ]	atemberaubend, großartig
to make a speech [tʊ ˌmeɪk ə 'spiːtʃ]	eine Rede halten
spices ['spaɪsɪz]	Gewürze
spider web ['spaɪdəweb]	Spinnennetz
spook [spuːk]	Gespenst
spoon [spuːn]	Löffel
spoonful ['spuːnfʊl]	ein Löffel (voll)
to sprinkle [tʊ 'sprɪŋkl]	bestreuen

spur-of-the-moment [ˌspɜ:rˌəvˌðə ˈməʊmənt] — spontan

square [skweə] — Platz

squash (AE) [skwɑ:ʃ] — Kürbis

to squeeze [tʊ skwi:z] — drücken, quetschen

sticky [ˈstɪkɪ] — stickig

strange [streɪndʒ] — seltsam, merkwürdig

strenuous [ˈstrenjʊəs] — anstrengend

to stretch one's legs [tʊ ˌstretʃ wʌnzˌˈlegz] — sich die Beine vertreten

strip [strɪp] — Streifen

stuffing [ˈstʌfɪŋ] — Füllung

sturdy [ˈstɜ:dɪ] — stabil, robust

to subdue sth [tʊ səbˈdju:ˌsʌmθɪŋ] — etw. unter Kontrolle bringen, unterdrücken

sub-standard [ˌsʌbˈstændəd] — unterdurchschnittlich, minderwertig

successful [səkˈsesfʊl] — erfolgreich

suffering from [ˈsʌfərɪŋ frəm] — leiden an

suit [su:t] — Anzug, Kostüm

supernatural (adj.) [ˌsu:pəˈnætʃərəl] — übernatürlich

superstitious [ˌsu:pəˈstɪʃəs] — abergläubisch

to support [tʊ səˈpɔ:t] — unterstützen

supporter [səˈpɔ:tə] — Befürworter(in)

to survive [tʊ səˈvaɪv] — überleben

sweltering [ˈsweltərɪŋ] — sehr heiß

to switch [tʊ swɪtʃ] — wechseln

to symbolize [tʊ ˈsɪmbəlaɪz] — symbolisieren

T

to take sth for granted [tʊ teɪk ˌsʌmθɪŋ fə ˈgrɑ:ntɪd] — etw. für selbstverständlich halten

takeaway [ˈteɪkəweɪ] — Essen zum Mitnehmen

taut [tɔ:t] — gespannt

taxes [ˈtæksɪz] — Steuern

techie [ˈtekɪ] — Technikfanatiker(in)

terrified [ˈterəfaɪd] — erschrocken, verängstigt

text message [ˈtekstˌmesɪdʒ] — SMS

thongs [θɒŋz] — Sandalen, Zehentrenner

thought [θɔ:t] — Gedanke

thoughtful [ˈθɔ:tfʊl] — nachdenklich

to throw away [tʊ θrəʊˌəˈweɪ] — wegwerfen

tile [taɪl] — Fliese

time capsule [ˈtaɪmˌkæpsju:l] — Kassette mit Zeitdokumenten

tin whistle [ˌtɪnˈwɪsl] — Blechflöte

tiny [ˈtaɪnɪ] — winzig

toothbrush [ˈtu:θbrʌʃ] — Zahnbürste

to touch [tʊ tʌtʃ] — berühren

touch wood [ˌtʌtʃˈwʊd] — Toi, toi, toi!

to trade [tʊ treɪd] — handeln

trader [ˈtreɪdə] — Händler(in)

to treasure [tʊ ˈtreʒə] — schätzen

treasure [ˈtreʒə] — Schatz

treatment [ˈtri:tmənt] — Behandlung

tremendous [trɪˈmendəs] — enorm, riesig

tribe [traɪb] — Stamm

trickster [ˈtrɪkstə] — Betrüger(in), Schwindler(in)

tricky [ˈtrɪkɪ] — knifflig, raffiniert

to tumble [tʊ ˈtʌmbl] — fallen, stürzen

turkey [ˈtɜ:kɪ] — Truthahn

24/7 twenty-four seven [ˌtwentɪfɔ:ˈsevn] — 24 Stunden am Tag, sieben Tage in der Woche

to twitter [tʊ ˈtwɪtə] — zwitschern

U

unbearably (adv.) [ʌnˈbeərəblɪ] — unausstehlich

unemployment [ˌʌnɪmˈplɔɪmənt] — Arbeitslosigkeit

unexpected (adj.) [ˌʌnɪkˈspektɪd] — unerwartet

unexpectedly (adv.) [ˌʌnɪkˈspektɪdlɪ] — unerwartet

unfortunately [ʌnˈfɔ:tʃənətlɪ] — leider

unhealthy [ʌnˈhelθɪ] — ungesund

uninvited (person) [ˌʌnɪnˈvaɪtɪd] — ungeladen

unique [ju:ˈni:k] — einmalig

unless [ənˈles] — es sei denn

unnecessary [ʌnˈnesəsərɪ] — überflüssig, unnötig

unrealistic [ˌʌnrɪəˈlɪstɪk] — unrealistisch

unusual [ʌnˈju:ʒʊəl] — ungewöhnlich

useful [ˈju:sfʊl] — nützlich, praktisch

usefulness [ˈju:sfʊlnəs] — Nützlichkeit, Brauchbarkeit

utility vehicle [ju:ˈtɪlətɪ ˌvɪəkl] — Mehrzweckfahrzeug

V

vandalism [ˈvændəlɪzm] — Vandalismus

to vanish [tʊ ˈvænɪʃ] — verschwinden

vein [veɪn] — Ader

Velcro [ˈvelkrəʊ] — Klettverschluss

venue [ˈvenju:] — Austragungsort

violence [ˈvaɪələns] — Gewalt

to volunteer [tʊ ˌvɒlənˈtɪə] — ehrenamtlich mitarbeiten

volunteer [ˌvɒlənˈtɪə] — ehrenamtliche(r) Mitarbeiter(in)

W

wage earner [ˈweɪdʒˌɜ:nə] — Lohnempfänger(in)

wardrobe [ˈwɔ:drəʊb] — Garderobe

waste of (money, time) [ˈweɪstˌəv (ˌmʌnɪ, ˌtaɪm)] — Geld-/Zeitverschwendung

to wear out [tʊ wearˌˈaʊt] — abtragen, abnutzen

weatherproof [ˈweðəpru:f] — wetterfest

wedding [ˈwedɪŋ] — Hochzeit

white lie [ˌwaɪtˌˈlaɪ] — harmlose Lüge

wide [waɪd] — breit

willingness [ˈwɪlɪŋnəs] — Bereitschaft (etw. zu tun)

to wind down [tʊ waɪndˌˈdaʊn] — entspannen, abspannen

wine-tasting [ˈwaɪnˌteɪstɪŋ] — Weinprobe

wise [waɪz] — klug, weise

witch [wɪtʃ] — Hexe

witness [ˈwɪtnəs] — Zeuge, Trauzeuge (-zeugin)

working conditions [ˈwɜ:kɪŋˌkənˌdɪʃnz] — Arbeitsbedingungen

worn [wɔ:n] — verschlissen

worthwhile [ˌwɜ:θˈwaɪl] — lohnend

wreath [ri:θ] — Kranz

to wrinkle [tʊ ˈrɪnkl] — zerknittern

wrinkle [ˈrɪnkl] — Falte

Y

yam (African vegetable) [jæm] — Jamswurzel

You're kidding! [ˌjɔ:ˌˈkɪdɪŋ] — Das ist doch wohl nicht dein Ernst!

yummy [ˈjʌmɪ] — lecker

Z

zip (BE), zipper (AE) [zɪp] [ˈzɪpər] — Reißverschluss

Quellennachweis